LIFE AND TIMES
OF RAGE

The Story Of A Force Recon Marine Mentoring Our Youth

Written By David Donald James

Edited By Jaime Lyn Acker

Edited by Jaime Lyn Acker

This is a work of non-fiction. Events, individuals, and locations are portrayed truthfully to the best of the author's memory. Some names may have been changed to respect privacy.

Paperback ISBN: 979-8-9937573-0-8
Published by Jaime Acker Publishing

Author's Note

This Story Almost Stayed Buried

If you're holding this book, I want you to know—it almost never happened.

Years ago, I spent about a year and a half writing down my experiences. I had a deep desire to document what I'd been through and hopefully pass along something that could inspire others. But after pouring everything out, the project sat untouched for years. Life got busy, and like so many things, it faded into the background.

Then something unexpected happened.

I was sharing a few stories from my time in the military with my longtime friend Jaime Acker, and she said something that struck a chord: "This sounds like something that should be a book—or even a movie." When I told her I had, in fact, written it all down years ago, she didn't hesitate. She offered to take a look.

That moment was the spark that reignited the fire.

Jaime didn't just read it—she jumped in with both feet. With her support, skill, and vision, what was once a dusty collection of memories began to transform into a real book. Her belief in the project gave it structure, clarity, and heart. Without her, it would still be sitting in a folder, unread and unfinished.

This journey has been humbling. It reminds me that sometimes it just takes one person to see value in what you've been through to bring it to life.

Thank you, Jaime, for helping me turn this story into something others can hold, read, and hopefully be inspired by. Your role in this project has been unforgettable.

With gratitude,

David Donald James

Table of Contents

Dedication

Dedicated to the brave souls lost during a dark day for 1st Force Reconnaissance Company (FMF): the tragic helicopter crash aboard the **USNS Pecos** on December 9, 1999. We honor the memory of:

- **GySgt James Paige**
- **SSgt Vince Sabasteanski**
- **SSgt David Galloway**
- **SSgt Jeffery Starling**
- **SSgt. William C. Dame, EOD**
- **HM1 Jay Asis**
- **Cpl Mark Baca**

These Marines, some of our nation's finest, may be gone, but they will never be forgotten.

1st Force Reconnaissance Marines, December 1999

In memory of those who gave all.

"Fear is a reaction.... Courage is a destination of the Warrior"

Acknowledgments

This book would not have come to life without the unwavering support and guidance of many. I would especially like to thank **Jaime Lyn Acker**, whose editorial insight, dedication, and belief in this project helped shape my story into a clear and powerful message.

Thank you to my family, fellow Marines, mentors, and every young person I've had the honor to mentor, you are the reason for this mission.

The Author, Dave "Rage" James.

Introduction

Every life has a story, but some stories are meant to be shared. Not for recognition, but for a greater purpose. This is my story. My life has been a journey through valleys of testing, tragedy, and resilience. Now, standing in my sixties, I can look back with clarity and conviction. Through it all, one truth has become undeniably clear to me: God was there, even when I couldn't see it.

Deciding to write this book didn't come lightly. For years, my experiences stayed locked away, known only to me and a select few. From the adrenaline-filled missions of my military days to the life-altering challenges and near-death experiences, each moment carried lessons that shaped me into the man I am today. But as I reflected on my journey, I realized my story wasn't just my own, it was meant to inspire, guide, and encourage others, especially the next generation.

Today, I have the privilege of serving as a mentor to troubled youth on a military base. It's my way of giving back, of sharing the lessons I've learned along the way. I don't yell or bark orders; that's not my approach. Instead, I stand strong as an example, a man who's faced life's darkest hours and emerged stronger, not because of my own strength, but because of the grace of God.

My testimony is a testament to God's glory and the transformative power of faith. I've come to understand that the trials I endured, from the training grounds to the personal struggles, were not without purpose. They were part of a divine plan that was unfolding, even when I couldn't see it.

Each near-death experience, every moment of doubt, and all the victories and failures were leading me to a greater understanding of who God is and the purpose He has for my life.

Through this book, I hope to share not just my story, but the hope and faith that have guided me through it. My journey wasn't easy, but it was worth it, and my greatest desire is for others to see that no matter how hard the road may seem, there is a light that can guide you through it. That light is the Lord Jesus Christ.

This book isn't just a recounting of events; it's a reflection on how faith can transform even the most challenging experiences into a testimony of resilience and purpose. My hope is to reach young people who are searching for direction, struggling with their own battles, or feeling like they're walking through life alone. I want you to know that you are not alone. God is there, just as He was there for me, and He has a plan for your life too.

As you read these pages, my hope is you'll see the hand of God weaving through the moments of my life, the good, the bad, and the unimaginable. It is a story of redemption, grace, and unshakable faith. And it is proof that even when we don't realize it, God is working, guiding, and carrying us through. My prayer is that my story will not only inspire you but also draw you closer to the One who makes all things possible.

Prologue: One Team, One Fight

The journey of a Marine is not just about missions and medals; it's about resilience, sacrifice, and the unbreakable bond of brotherhood. My path was forged in the crucible of grueling missions, personal loss, and the pursuit of a higher purpose. These moments shaped who I am today and taught me lessons I hoped to pass on to the next generation of warriors-lessons that, I now understand, were part of a divine plan guiding me through every trial.

This book is a testament to those lessons. It's not just a recounting of challenges overcome and milestones reached; it's a guide for those who face their own struggles, whether in the military or in life. As I shared in the introduction, my journey is a testimony to God's grace and resilience. Through these pages, I hope to inspire the next generation to find their strength, embrace their purpose, and rise to meet their challenges, knowing they are never alone.

From surviving a frigid open-water swim off the coast of San Clemente Island to enduring the most brutal initiation ceremony of my career, these stories are more than memories, they are steppingstones placed by God to mold me into the man I am today. Each moment taught me grit, determination, and the power of never giving up, even in the darkest hours.

Every chapter in this story is a step in a journey of transformation. It is a story of perseverance, faith, and the unshakable bond of brotherhood. I invite you to walk alongside me, to face the challenges, and to find the strength within yourself to overcome. Together, we will see how, even in life's most difficult moments, God is always there, guiding us toward a greater purpose.

Chapter 1

Young Dave "Rage" James

I was born in Warren, Ohio, in the early 1960s and spent my earliest years in Lordstown, where much of my dad's side of the family lived. My grandparents had a farm, a rugged spread of land with rusted fences, creaking barns, and muddy fields that turned to ice in the winter. That farm became my kingdom. I ran wild through the cornfields and pastures with my two sisters and cousins, often barefoot, always untamed. You could hear our laughter echoing off the silo walls like a wild pack claiming its territory. Even then, people would say, "That boy's headed for the military." And they weren't wrong.

I had a butch haircut, a box of plastic army men I treated like real soldiers, and fists that were always balled up, ready for action. There was a kind of storm in me, something loud, fast, and dangerous, like a racecar with no brakes.

Once, when I was just a little kid, I gave my baby sister a bath using an entire box of Tide laundry detergent. Bubbles overflowed the tub and spread across the floor like chemical warfare. In my mind, I was on a cleaning mission, scrubbing in like a Corpsman on a combat op. My mom didn't quite see it that way, but even she had to laugh once the panic wore off. That wild energy never left me, it just evolved. I thought I was helping to make sure she was really clean! Looking back, it was one of those moments that defined my wild and unrelenting energy.

When I was three, my family moved to Minnesota. That's where I grew up, surrounded by a world of fast cars and adrenaline. My dad was a, part of the legendary James Gang Racing Team. His car, *The Spirit of '76*, looked like a rocket with wheels—painted in deep purple, red, white, and blue, with a roaring 440-cubic-inch big-block engine that could rattle your bones from fifty feet away. That car wasn't just metal and paint, it was a symbol. It was *him*. Grit, fire, and speed. I idolized every bit of it.

As a kid, I was intense and focused, always aiming to do my best. But I also had a wild streak. Bullies always seemed to find me in a crowd. Bullies were drawn to me like flies to blood—not because I was weak, but because I was *volatile*. They didn't dare mess with me directly, but they loved pushing my buttons, and they usually got what they came for. One second, I'd be calm, the next I was throwing punches like I was clearing a room in a hostile village. They lit the fuse and stood back to watch the fireworks.

I spent every chance I had with my dad, whether it was tagging along to his job, hanging out in the race car garage, or going to the track. The garage was filled with tough, no-nonsense guys, just like my dad, and that's where I picked up a lot of my toughness. It wasn't a place for feelings, it was a place for fire, grease, and grit. My dad didn't tolerate weakness, and neither did I.

I had a reputation for being quick to throw down. If someone disrespected me or picked on someone weaker, I didn't talk, I just started swinging. My fists did the talking, and they spoke fluent "hell no." I wasn't a bully, but I had zero patience for anyone who preyed on the weak. My mom tried her best to manage my wild energy, but it wasn't easy for her. She was there for me as much as she could be, but I was too restless, too angry. Even as a kid, I could see the unfairness in the world, the way people hurt others or took advantage of them, and it made me confused and furious. I didn't have the words to explain it then, but I felt it burning under my skin. Like my soul was wearing a uniform before my body ever did.

Growing up wasn't easy. My family moved nine times, which meant nine different schools. Starting over that many times made it hard to form lasting friendships, and each new school brought its own set of bullies. I had to keep proving myself, over and over again. Every new hallway was a battlefield, and I learned early: don't flinch, don't fold, don't back down.

By the time we moved to Apple Valley during my high school years, I was already on the edge. Without my dad around much, I started to spiral, slowly turning into a full-blown hellraiser. Apple Valley became the perfect environment for my rebellious energy, and it didn't take long before I embraced the chaos. I didn't find the fire—I *became* it.

Looking back now, I can see that even in those wild years, God's hand was at work. I didn't realize it at the time, but those chaotic experiences were shaping me. The lessons in resilience, toughness, and survival would become essential to who I am today, and they remind me that there was always a greater plan unfolding, even when I couldn't see it. It's clear to me now that He had a plan for me, even when I didn't have one for myself.

God doesn't always speak in silence—sometimes He roars through broken glass and burned bridges.

It's clear to me now that He had a plan for me, even when I didn't have one for myself.

Chapter 2

From Bloomington to Apple Valley – A Wild Ride

I grew up in Bloomington, Minnesota, across from the Met Center, where the Minnesota Vikings, Twins, and North Stars played. Back then, the area wasn't the Mall of America it is today. The air always carried the scent of fresh-cut grass and spilled popcorn, and on game nights, you could hear distant roars echoing like thunder. Life took a turn at sixteen when, in the summer of 1979, we moved to Apple Valley, a picturesque suburb with apple trees in every backyard. Apple Valley, located 20 miles from Minneapolis, was a place where the wealthy fled the city for quiet comfort.

Not long after moving, I found myself driving my dad's brand-new 1979 Chevy Silverado to pick up a part for our family's James Gang Racing Team. The engine rumbled beneath me like a beast, and as the summer wind tangled through my hair, I felt freedom on the open road. That's when I first met two hitchhikers on Highway 42—Dan and Brady—who would later become my best friends. I dropped them off at McDonald's, not realizing that our paths were destined to cross again.

Making a Name for Myself

In August, I started my first day at Apple Valley Senior High School. As the new kid, I didn't know anyone besides Dan and Brady. In gym class, the quarterback on my own team deliberately threw a football at my back multiple times and clipped me during plays. The sound of the ball hitting my spine echoed like a war drum, and my blood boiled with each hit. When he tried it again, I snapped. Tackling him to the ground, I bloodied his nose before gym classmates could pull us apart. By lunchtime, word had spread that I had fought and beaten one of the most popular kids in school.

Surprisingly, his brother, rumored to seek revenge, turned out to be a kind guy who became a friend. Soon enough, the tough kids took notice of me. I earned a reputation as a fighter, and the school's legendary wrestling team brought me on board. Wrestling became my outlet as I competed in the junior varsity 132-pound weight class. Every slam onto the mat was like exorcising a demon I didn't even know I had.

The Hell Raisers and the James Gang

Around this time, Brady and I reunited, forging a friendship filled with reckless adventures: drinking, fighting, chasing girls, and causing trouble across Dakota County. We became known as the Hell Raisers—a wild tag team of chaos in a town too quiet for our fire.

My dad's racing career kept him away most weekends, and when he wasn't racing with the ASA Late Model Series, he worked for a roofing company in Minneapolis. Despite his absence, my dad sometimes brought me to the race garage, where I swept floors, cleaned tools, and absorbed the culture of the crew. Wrenches clanked, engines revved, and cigarette smoke swirled through the air like a mechanic's incense.

On race weekends, my family would cheer him on

from the bleachers, enjoying popcorn and Coke as he consistently placed in the top five. Afterward, the pits buzzed with camaraderie and beer—Pabst Blue Ribbon, Schlitz, and Hamms were the favorites.

The post-race tradition included heading to Dino's Bar in Elko, where pit crews, drivers, and their families gathered. At thirteen, my younger sister and I would swipe leftover beers from tables. It was a wild introduction to adulthood. The jukebox played Hank Williams and Springsteen while laughter and lies flowed freely.

One night after a race, I wandered down a dark dirt road and encountered two men who assaulted me over a supposed racing-related grudge. Their fists fell like bricks. A woman in their group begged them to stop, saving me from worse injuries.

Rebellion and Consequences

With my dad often away, I rebelled hard. I fought often, drank heavily, and earned the ire of Apple Valley's school district. I was infamous for mooning the entire school during an Apple Valley Eagles AAA state game, which finally got me expelled.

A family counselor tried intervening, but I told her to leave.

"This ain't therapy," I said, slamming the door. "It's survival."

She did, and never came back. Soon after, I was no longer welcome at home. With little money, I boarded a bus to Florida, only to return shortly after. Brady's family took me in, introducing me to a more disciplined environment in their upscale Palomino Estates home. Their rules felt like shackles at first, but I slowly realized it was structure, not punishment, I'd been missing.

A Lesson in Reflection

Despite my antics, I excelled at art. My English teacher, who was a Korean War veteran, offered me a C grade if I built a guillotine. Inspired, I designed and built one out of wood, metal, and rope, complete with red paint for effect. Proud of my creation, I delivered it to the teacher, who displayed it on top of his filing cabinet.

Two years later, while visiting the school, I saw the guillotine still sitting there.

That's when it hit me: the guillotine symbolized my self-destructive behavior. I had been metaphorically "cutting off my own head" with my actions.

The Turning Point

Looking back, my wild years in Apple Valley shaped me in ways I didn't fully understand at the time. Joining the wrestling team after standing up for myself in gym class gave me confidence. My dad's racing career instilled resilience and a fierce competitive spirit. Even my chaotic, rebellious adventures left me with lessons in perseverance, camaraderie, and survival that I carried into adulthood.

Now, with the clarity that comes from years of reflection, I can see how God's hand was at work, even then. He was guiding me through those turbulent years, using every challenge and every misstep to prepare me for what was to come. While I didn't know Him then, I can look back and see that He was there, shaping me and planting the seeds of resilience, strength, and faith that would carry me forward.

These lessons, though painful and wild, became the foundation for the man I would become.

"Sometimes you have to burn down the orchard to see how strong your roots really are."

Chapter 3

Babes Bar Room Fight

Leaving the Marines and landing in jail at Dakota County Jail, MN, for one year, that's not how I imagined my transition back to civilian life. Just eleven days out of Force Recon, I found myself in a situation that would change everything.

It started innocently enough. My lifelong friend Brady and I decided to have a few drinks on a Saturday afternoon at Babes Bar in Lakeville, MN. We were enjoying ourselves, catching up, and sharing laughs with two women who had joined us. It felt good to be home, out of the Marines, and surrounded by friends. But things took a sharp turn when Keith, a local restaurant owner I'd never met, decided to make me his target.

As I stood at the bar, talking and having a drink, Keith came up behind me and hit me hard in the back with his elbow. I let it go the first time, chalking it up to a mistake or a bad joke. But ten minutes later, he did it again. Still, I ignored it. Then, about twenty minutes after that, he escalated. Keith shoved me into a booth, knocking me onto the two women I was sitting with. That was it. Eleven days out of the Corps, and my instincts as a Special Operations soldier kicked in. I came out of that booth and took Keith to the ground.

The moment my back hit that booth, something snapped. Not out of anger—but from years of conditioning. You don't hesitate in the field. You act, or someone gets hurt.

The fight didn't last long, and I got the better of him. But as they say, I might have won the fight, but I lost in the end. While it was self-defense at first, I was told I went beyond the line of what was necessary. That night ended with me being charged, and eventually, I was sentenced to one year in Dakota County Jail.

The cuffs felt heavier than they should've. Not because of their weight—but because of what they meant. I wasn't a Marine in that moment. I was an inmate.

During my time in jail, I had a lot of time to reflect on what had happened. One thing I'll never forget is how I remained positive despite everything. I didn't know the Lord Jesus back then, but as I look back now, I can clearly see that God was with me the whole time. He gave me strength and clarity when I needed it most, even when I didn't realize it. That year in jail became a period of growth and reckoning. I took full responsibility for my actions, knowing that my training and instincts, while invaluable in the field, had to be tempered in civilian life.

I wasn't behind bars—I was inside a mirror. And every day, I had to face what I saw. No medals. No rank. Just a man learning who he was outside the uniform.

I completed my court-ordered sentencing and worked hard to make amends. Over time, I put it all behind me, and the judge restored all my rights. But more importantly, I came to understand that God had a hand in guiding me through that storm, shaping me into the person I'm proud to be today.

Pain has a way of pruning pride. And humility, when earned the hard way, is a better teacher than any drill instructor.

This chapter of my life taught me the importance of accountability and faith. While I can't change the past, I've learned to face the consequences of my actions head-on and move forward with purpose, integrity, and gratitude for the unseen presence that carried me through.

A life of hard training teaches you how to survive. But a jail cell teaches you how to live. One forged my body. The other shaped my soul.

Chapter 4

U.S. Army Green Beret Robert P. Mose

After an unexceptional high school career which I completed in the early 1980s, I joined the U.S. Army as a Combat Engineer (Military Occupational Specialty 12C). I completed basic training at Fort Leonard Wood, Missouri, and was assigned to Echo Company in the 8th Engineer Battalion in Mannheim, Germany. The cold steel of winter clung to the base, and the grey skies seemed to echo the grit of the training ground.

Our First Sergeant was Robert P. Mose, a highly decorated soldier who had completed three tours of duty in Vietnam with highly specialized units known as MACV (Special Forces Green Beret). He was from Minnesota and rode a 1979 Harley Davidson Roadster with "Milwaukee Iron" painted on the gas tank. The roar of that bike became a signal of intensity and reverence. Prior to becoming our First Sergeant, he had been stationed in Germany with the 10th Special Forces Group for six years. Although he was 55 years old, he was physically intimidating and incredibly motivating.

As an Airborne Ranger, he set an example for others to follow. Despite being 55, he was in better condition than many members of the company who were more than 30 years younger, and he conducted PT (physical training) with the company every morning.

"You want to fight like warriors? Then train like

inferno," he'd order, sweat rolling off his brow in the dawn light. "Nobody's carrying you to glory."

He made it known that he liked me because I was motivated and knew my job well. He always encouraged me to try harder, to do better, and to look for bigger opportunities. His mentorship planted the seed, my first real interest in the elite Army Special Forces.

During the 26 months I was stationed as a Combat Engineer in Europe, our unit spent a lot of time training on the Rhine River. The water shimmered with morning mist, and we often moved silently along its edge, blending into the fog like ghosts. I was able to travel throughout Germany where I enjoyed the beautiful countryside containing grape vineyards as well as the pubs and guest houses. Frankfurt's red-light district was a wild place—sex, drugs, and rock-and-roll were at their peak. I didn't touch drugs, but I drank enough to drown my youth.

While stationed at Fort Hood, Texas, I bought a 1979 Harley Davidson Sportster from Armadillo Custom Motorcycle Shop. I became a regular in every biker bar I could find. The rumble of the engine was my escape, and the bars became my battlegrounds. I continued to be a hell-raiser and hung out in every Biker Bar I could find. I wasn't just chasing wind," I used to joke. "I was chasing adrenaline—with a chaser of whiskey."

My experience in the Army was a great time, especially serving in Europe for 2 1/2 years, But deep down, I wanted more. I wanted a challenge that would break me and build me again. Being a Combat Engineer in the US

Army just wasn't filling my desire to excel, so I chose not to reenlist and left the Army after my commitment ended.

Less than a year later, I needed fire again, so I enlisted in the United States Marine Corps. I was in phenomenal shape and mentally sharper than ever. I was sent from Oshkosh, Wisconsin to United States Marine Corps Bootcamp at Marine Corps Recruit Depot (MCRD) San Diego, California

After earning the coveted Eagle, Globe, and Anchor, I headed to the School of Infantry at Camp Pendleton, California. While learning the skills necessary to function as an infantry Marine, I was afforded the opportunity to attempt the Recon Indoc to earn a position in the elite Marine Corps Reconnaissance community.

I learned the basic duties and responsibilities of a Reconnaissance Marine, as well as patrolling techniques and different insertion and extraction methods which enable small teams of Marines to operate behind enemy lines in order to be "the eyes and ears" of the Marine Division Commanders.

I later transferred to Bravo Company at 3rd Reconnaissance Battalion in Okinawa, Japan. Bravo Company was designated as the Counter Terrorist, or Direct-Action Platoon. I completed additional specialized training where I learned to participate as a member of platoon sized elements which conducted close quarters battles, breaching and room clearing, and also continued to improve patrolling and insertion/extraction techniques.

After approximately three years at 3rd Recon

Battalion, I transferred to 7th Platoon at 1st Force Reconnaissance Company at Los Flores, Camp Pendleton, California where I remained until the end of my service. While Battalion Recon works for the Marine Division Commanders, Force Reconnaissance works for the Marine Expeditionary Force (MEF), focusing on deep reconnaissance (further behind enemy lines) and work for the MEF Commander.

My time in the Marine Corps was very fulfilling. Being in the special operations community, constantly being challenged and obtaining a physical fitness level that I never could have imagined gave me the confidence and a mental fortitude that helped push me through any challenges. I was highly motivated and took on every challenge with excitement and anticipation of pushing the envelope of mind and body. I realized, "Pain didn't break me, it introduced me to who I really was."

During my time in the military, I was able to travel around the world. I was in 22 different countries, and I found that I had a unique experience learning about the different cultures and seeing their beautiful landscape in every country. In Perth, Australia I worked with Australian Special Air Service (SAS) for three weeks. I especially enjoyed watching and learning about rugby. The Aussies had a rough exterior and stood tall and confident, which was very similar to the Recon Marines I worked with and I found to be very healthy to be around. On numerous occasions, we also worked alongside U.S. Navy SEALs and U.S. Army Special Forces. During my time serving in the military, I developed a can-do attitude and never quit culture. I learned to embrace every moment and focus on the task of the day. I was surrounded by positive people who were always trying to achieve more, which I carried with me after I left the military. In all the trials and tribulations I have encountered, no matter how hard they were, I have pushed through and came out even more prepared for future challenges. The more I experienced and the more I went through I realized that a higher power was always with me, protecting me and giving me courage, the strength, and the will to trust and believe. God's been walking with me this whole time," I realized. "Even when I thought I was running alone. I have continued to work hard, kept faith, and surrounded myself with people who I could trust who were trying to do better themselves and motivating me to do better as well. The path to purpose is paved in grit, faith, and fire.

Chapter 5
My Longest, Coldest Combat Swim

The ocean is an unforgiving place. It doesn't negotiate. It devours the unprepared and humbles the brave. It doesn't care about your training, your gear, or your willpower. In February 1988, I learned just how brutal it could be when my team faced one of the coldest, longest swims of our lives a mission that would test our endurance, teamwork, and resolve.

We were aboard the USS Ogden, preparing for our Final Training Exercise (FTX) with SEAL Team One off San Clemente Island. The wind howled across the deck, carrying the scent of salt and diesel as whitecaps shattered in the distance. The mission was straightforward in design but brutal in execution: a high-speed cast from a Navy Sea Fox boat into freezing waters, followed by a combative swim to the island, where we'd establish an Observation Point (OP). It wasn't just a test of skill, it was a test of will.

The Sea Fox was a compact, high-speed craft designed for waterborne operations, with 900-horsepower twin diesel engines that roared like thunder over the waves. Inside its 36-foot frame, my six-man Marine Recon team huddled tightly, trying to stay warm in the biting wind. The Pacific in February is merciless, with water temperatures barely climbing above 56 degrees, and we didn't have wetsuits. We were dressed in camouflage fatigues, jungle boots, and dive socks. The cold wasn't just uncomfortable it was dangerous.

"You ready for this?" I asked my swim buddy, trying to mask the tension in my voice. He smirked, teeth already chattering. "Do I have a choice?"

As we neared the drop-off point under the cover of darkness, the crew chief gave the one-minute warning. The hum of the engines and the bite of diesel fumes filled the air as I ran through my final equipment checks: UDT vest secured, rucksack tied tightly, dive mask ready, rocket fins strapped. At the thirty-second mark, my heart pounded in sync with the roar of the Sea Fox's engines. Spray lashed our faces as the bow rose and slammed against the black water. When the green light flashed, I stepped off the boat at 32 knots, plunging into the icy void.

The shock of the freezing water stole my breath, and for a moment, I was disoriented, submerged 15 feet below the surface. Training kicked in, and I surfaced quickly, gasping as the cold bit into my skin. The ocean rollers were three feet high, making it nearly impossible to see, but one by one, we regrouped in the darkness.

Our team leader gave us a silent command with a look that needed no words: Grab your swim buddy and start moving. I paired up with my swim buddy, who was already struggling. His teeth chattered violently, the sound carrying over the waves.

The cold seeped into our bones, slowing our movements and tightening our muscles. Every inch forward felt like a negotiation with death, a trade of pain for progress. Within minutes, hypothermia began to take hold, but there was no time to dwell on it. Giving up wasn't an option.

We swam relentlessly, every stroke feeling heavier than the last. The Sea Fox had dropped us much farther than expected, nearly 3,200 meters from the shore. The island was invisible, hidden by the massive rollers and the pitch-black sky. But we kept moving. Out loud, I repeated the same words to myself and my swim buddy: "Keep kicking. Don't stop."

The minutes stretched into what felt like hours. The Pacific became a cruel adversary, fighting us at every turn. Finally, I heard the faint crash of surf against the shore. Relief surged through me as we approached the seven-foot waves of the surf zone.

"Almost there," I gasped, pushing harder. Exhausted but determined, we dove under the waves, inching closer to the beach. Every second felt like an eternity.

When we reached the sand, it felt like victory. My body was numb, my muscles trembling with exhaustion, but we had made it. As we regrouped, our Team Leader gave the order to change into dry uniforms and prepare for the next phase. The reconnaissance portion of the mission was scrapped due to our condition. Instead, we moved straight to establishing the Observation Point.

During the debrief, our Team Leader took full responsibility for the lack of wetsuits. It was a hard lesson but an invaluable one. That night in the Pacific pushed us beyond our physical and mental limits. I left part of myself in that water, and what emerged was forged in something colder and stronger than steel. It forced us to rely on our training, on each other, and on the sheer will to survive.

Looking back, that mission wasn't just a test of endurance, it was a turning point. It reminded me that no challenge is insurmountable with the right mindset and a team you can trust. Now, with the benefit of years and perspective, I see it as more than just a lesson in survival. I see God's hand in it all, teaching me resilience and revealing a deeper purpose. That frigid swim was just one of many moments where God was quietly shaping me, preparing me for the battles ahead. It's a reminder that even in the most brutal conditions, we are never truly alone.

Chapter 6
Military Special Operations Airborne Jumps That Didn't Quite Go As Planned

1986: Jump School at Fort Benning

The first step in my airborne journey began at Fort Benning, Georgia. Assigned to Alpha Company, I was one of the few Marines among the Army-dominated ranks. My roster number, N132, marked me as Marine personnel in a sea of soldiers. As I stood on the tarmac, hearing the command, "Hook up!" echo through the aircraft, the reality of what lay ahead hit me.

The door of the C-130 Hercules opened, the wind roaring at 130 knots, hitting us with a force that rattled both nerves and confidence. Inside, the air was tense with anticipation as we shuffled toward the door. "Keep your head on a swivel, Marine," the jumpmaster barked. "One wrong move and you'll meet the earth harder than you want to." One by one, we stepped out into the void, the roar of the engines replaced by the rush of wind and the stunning realization of freefall. Descending 1,250 feet to the ground, my heart raced, each moment feeling both exhilarating and surreal.

The three-week Basic Airborne Course was relentless. Ground week focused on the fundamentals, meticulously donning equipment, executing mock door exercises dozens of times, and repeatedly practicing parachute landing falls. The drills were designed to instill muscle memory, and they pushed us past our breaking points to ensure we could operate under pressure. The 34-foot tower forced us to confront and conquer our fear of heights, and every successful jump brought a mix of pride and relief. "You land like you train," our instructor reminded us. "So you train like you mean it."

By the time I earned my U.S. Army Parachutist Wings, I wasn't just more skilled, I was more prepared for the realities of what lay ahead. The constant drilling had built a confidence that would serve as my foundation for the trials to come, both in the air and on the ground.

Combat Jumps and Water Training

Returning to my Recon unit, the stakes were raised. Night combat jumps into 500-foot Above Ground Level (AGL) drop zones demanded precision, coordination, and absolute focus. Under the cover of darkness, with only the moonlight to guide us, every movement was calculated to avoid detection. As we exited the aircraft, the silence of the night was broken only by the rush of wind and the rustling of our parachutes. "No sound, no silhouette. We are shadows tonight," whispered our team lead just before we jumped. We couldn't afford to make a sound as we descended. The drop zones were tight and unforgiving, often surrounded by obstacles that could turn a small mistake into a deadly misstep.

Every jump was a test of survival, not just skill. The pressure to remain undetected heightened the stakes, and the smallest error could have catastrophic consequences.

Whether it was navigating unseen hazards on the ground or regrouping silently with the team, each jump taught us to trust in our training and rely on each other in ways that went far beyond the classroom. "If you miss the mark, you don't just get a do-over," one of the senior NCOs had warned. "You get a body bag." These missions weren't just exercises; they prepared us for the realities we might face in combat and the razor-thin margin between success and failure.

Water jumps brought new challenges. Training began in the base pool recon swim tank, an Olympic-sized pool where parachutes were stretched across its length. The task was simple in theory but grueling in execution: swim underwater in the 15-foot-deep section, locate the parachute's apex, and follow the stitching to escape. The drill simulated being trapped under a chute in water, a scenario that demanded calm focus.

My first water jump was unforgettable. Aboard a CH Sea Knight helicopter over the Pacific Ocean, I was first in the stick. As I stood on the ramp, waiting for the green light, I was unexpectedly knocked out of the aircraft. Spiraling through the air, I faced immediate problems: twisted risers and a partially deployed chute. Drawing on my training, I methodically resolved each issue. "One step at a time," I told myself. "Breathe. Fix the lines. Focus." When I hit the water, the impact was jarring, and the reality of being alone in the vast Pacific set in. Treading water, I prayed for rescue and tried to remain calm.

After what felt like hours, I heard the faint sound of boat engines. Relief surged as the rescue crew approached and pulled me aboard. During the debrief, I learned what had happened. One of my teammates had slipped on oil in the helicopter, accidentally pushing me out. The same incident caused his arm to get tangled in the suspension lines, leaving him with a torn bicep. "You both walked away," the corpsman said. "That's a win in my book." Both of us were lucky to have survived. Reflecting on that day, I realized how quickly things could go wrong and how vital it was to rely on training and faith to make it through.

Advanced Special Forces Training

Fort Bragg, North Carolina, became my proving ground. Completing the SFARTAETC (Special Forces Advanced Reconnaissance Target Analysis and Exploitation Techniques Course) pushed me to master close-quarters fight, hostage rescue, and counter-terrorism tactics. Ranger School followed, a grueling 61-day ordeal that tested every limit. With only one hour of sleep a night and a single MRE meal a day, I lost 20 pounds. Out of 483 students, only 168 graduated. **"You want that tab?" our instructor growled. "Then suffer for it."** Receiving my Black and Gold Ranger Tab was a hard-fought victory and remains something I am extremely proud I was able to accomplish.

Next was SERE School, a brutal test of survival, evasion, resistance, and escape. The training was relentless, designed to strip away every comfort and push you to your breaking point, both mentally and physically. From simulated capture and interrogation to surviving with nothing but your wits and limited resources, every moment felt like a test of whether you could endure the unthinkable. By the end, I had lost 15 pounds and carried a deep awareness of what true resilience meant.

One defining moment during SERE involved navigating dense forest terrain while evading capture, my body screaming from exhaustion. I remember the searing cold and the constant struggle to stay alert, knowing one misstep could lead to "interrogation" I wasn't sure I could endure. "You keep moving or they find you," I told myself. "Pain is temporary. Capture isn't." Every challenge in SERE wasn't just about survival tactics, it was about finding the strength to keep going when you thought you had none left. Those lessons became a cornerstone of my endurance, discipline, and the mental fortitude I would carry into every trial that lay ahead.

The Gold Wing Jump

The culmination of my training was my Gold Wing jump with the 82nd Airborne. Over 500 parachutists filled the sky, exiting C-130 Hercules aircraft in synchronized waves. The roar of the engines, the sight of parachutes blooming across the sky, and the adrenaline coursing through my veins created an unforgettable moment. The sheer magnitude of it all was breathtaking, but it demanded intense focus.

As I exited the aircraft, I quickly scanned my surroundings, ensuring I didn't collide with the other jumpers. Parachutes were everywhere, and the air was filled with the shouts of commands and the rush of wind. "Watch your airspace! Stack high to low!" came the voice from a nearby jumper. Amidst the beauty and chaos, I became momentarily distracted. My descent seemed faster than expected, and I failed to execute my parachute landing fall (PLF) properly. The ground came up hard and fast. The impact sent a shockwave through my body, leaving me stunned and gasping for air.

For a moment, I thought I had broken my femur. Pain radiated through my leg, and I braced myself for the worst. But as I assessed the damage, I realized that, by God's grace, I had avoided serious injury. Despite the rattling experience, I stood up, shook it off, and rejoined my unit, humbled by the power of preparation and a higher hand guiding my steps.

The challenges of airborne training taught me more than technical skills. They instilled discipline, resilience, and trust in both my training and a higher purpose. Each jump, from the base pool to the Pacific Ocean to the skies over Fort Bragg, was a trial that shaped me into who I am today.

As I headed to Okinawa for the Gold Wing Ceremony, I carried the weight of these experiences. They had prepared me for the next defining moment of my career, one that would test not only my physical endurance but also my unshakable faith.

In the end, it wasn't just about jumping out of planes. It was about standing up every time you hit the ground.

That's what being a warrior truly means.

The Author's Ranger School Graduation 7-89.

Chapter 7
Legacy On The Wrist: A Frogman's Gift

T here are moments in life when time itself seems to pause—when history, legacy, and personal connection all collide. For me, one of those moments came through a man named John Tegg and a watch that had witnessed the very birth of the Navy SEALs.

John Tegg isn't just a friend. He is one of the original Navy SEALs—a plank owner of SEAL Team Two. He received his Trident on January 1, 1962, from none other than President John F. Kennedy himself at North Fork Naval Base. That day marked the official establishment of the U.S. Navy SEALs. And on his wrist during that historic moment? A 1958 Submariner Oyster Rolex issued by Naval Special Warfare.

The watch was more than just a piece of gear. It was a witness to the beginning of something legendary. John wore it through his training evolutions, his deployments, and on the very day JFK handed him the sacred Trident that defined a new era of special operations.

Years later, our paths crossed under unexpected circumstances.

Back in 2007, I was living in Apple Valley, Minnesota. I trained regularly at Fitness 19 in Burnsville and would often ride my 1950s replica Schwinn beach cruiser the

20-mile round trip to and from the gym. One day after a workout, I stopped at a QuikTrip gas station to grab a Snickers bar. I was wearing a Special Ops T-shirt. The woman at the counter glanced at my shirt and told me her neighbor was a retired Navy SEAL. I must have rolled my eyes—everyone seems to "know a SEAL"—but she insisted. "His name is John Tegg. He goes to the SEAL reunions in Fort Pierce."

That caught my attention. I wrote down my number and told her to have him give me a call.

A few days later, John called. We arranged to meet at Apple Valley Senior High, where he was coaching the school's diving team. When I walked into the pool area, I saw a tall, stern, in-shape older man wearing a navy blue baseball cap with a small gold Trident on it. He was finishing up a coaching session, so I waited. When we finally shook hands, there was an immediate mutual respect—a bond between warriors from different generations.

From that day on, we met regularly at Caribou Coffee in Apple Valley or at Starbucks in Burnsville. Over those coffees, John began to share his stories—gritty, raw tales of the early Frogman days. He had joined the Navy after a year at the University of Minnesota on a swimming and diving scholarship. His goal had always been to become a UDT diver. After boot camp at Great Lakes, he was originally assigned to an air wing in Cocoa Beach, Florida. But he never gave up on his dream. He persistently requested a transfer to the elite UDT/BUDS course at Fort Pierce. Eventually, his request was granted.

John graduated with Class 23, one of only twelve to finish. He served with UDT-21 and was one of the first twelve men chosen for SEAL Team Two. On January 1, 1962, in front of JFK, John Tegg became the 45th Navy SEAL in U.S. history.

Fast-forward to just a couple years ago: I was telling John about a Rolex I was thinking of buying—a new Sea-Dweller Submariner. He paused and said, "I still have mine from '58. The one I was wearing when JFK gave us our Tridents."

The next morning, we met again. John laid the watch on the table along with black-and-white photos of him in uniform, standing proudly with President Kennedy. He told me about the dives, the training, the brotherhood—all while wearing that Rolex. And then, with no ceremony and no buildup, he said, "I want you to have it."

I was stunned. Humbled. Speechless.

"I have no one else to pass it to," he said. His wife had passed the year before, and he trusted me to carry on its legacy.

I posted about it briefly on social media. The post received over 300 comments and messages—many from SEALs and veterans. Offers came pouring in to buy it, but I wasn't interested. That watch isn't a collector's item. It's a symbol of sacrifice, courage, and trust. I'm not the owner of it. I'm just its guardian.

I've since contacted the U.S. Navy SEAL Museum in Fort Pierce about possibly donating it in the future. It deserves to be displayed where its story—and John's—can inspire generations to come.

John and I still meet for coffee when I'm in Apple Valley. I cherish his stories. They come from a time when men trained with knives in their teeth and fire in their hearts. A time when nothing was guaranteed, and everything had to be earned.

And every time I look at that Rolex, I remember the day JFK pinned the Trident on a young Frogman's chest and unknowingly passed a legacy down through generations. From that moment in 1962 to my wrist today, the heartbeat of Naval Special Warfare lives on.

"The only easy day was yesterday."

The Author and John Tegg, plank owner with
SEAL TEAM 2, January 1, 1962. The morning he passed
on his Naval Special Warfare-issued 1958 Submariner
Oyster Rolex to the author.

Chapter 8
Sgt. Jim "The Body" Burns Carrying The Torch For A Mentor, Brother, and Friend

Sgt. Jim Burns wasn't just my mentor and Marine Force Reconnaissance brother, he was a force of nature. Known affectionately as "The Body," Jim embodied physical strength, mental toughness, and an unwavering commitment to excellence. His tragic death was a devastating loss, but his legacy continues to inspire me and countless others. This chapter is dedicated to honoring his memory and the brotherhood we forged in our shared journey.

Meeting Jim "The Body" Burns

The first time I met Lance Corporal Jim Burns was in 1986 at 1st Reconnaissance Battalion, in the Quonset Hut gym. A sharp wind was howling outside, rattling the metal walls and adding a rhythmic backdrop to the sound of iron hitting the floor. He was working out with another reconnaissance Marine, his jet-black hair slicked back and his lean, muscular frame moving with precision. At just 21 years old, Jim was already building a reputation as an unstoppable Marine. Weighing around 170 pounds, he was a powerhouse who would outwork just about anyone.

Jim's physical abilities were legendary. He clocked an astonishing 14:30 run time on the Marine Corps Physical Fitness Test, a feat that few could match. But Jim wasn't just strong, he had a fiery intensity that commanded attention.

I remember partying with him at the Talega beer gardens a couple of times. The music was loud, the air filled with laughter and the buzz of Marine camaraderie. On more than one occasion, Jim's fiery nature would get the better of him, and it'd take a group of us to calm him down.

"Burns! Hey, easy, man," I'd shout, grabbing his arm as he clenched his jaw. "Save it for the field."

His strength was something you couldn't ignore. He was as strong as a bull, and every inch of him told the story of a warrior molded by fire.

Despite his occasional outbursts, Jim was a man of few words. When he spoke, he didn't waste breath. His confidence was unmatched and entirely natural, a quiet yet powerful presence that inspired respect.

Jim's Journey to Greatness

Jim's military journey began when he joined the United States Marine Corps at the age of 21. After successfully completing Marine Corps Boot Camp, he checked into the Infantry Training Battalion at the School of Infantry. It wasn't long before he took on the grueling Force Recon Indoctrination, earning his place among the elite.

Once Jim completed the Amphibious Reconnaissance Course (ARC) in Coronado, CA, he attended an array of specialized training programs. He became a master of skills like high-altitude, low-opening (HALO) parachuting, combat diving, hostage rescue, and more. Each training badge wasn't just a skill—it was a scar carved into time. Jim didn't collect qualifications; he collected thresholds most men never dared to cross.

These achievements earned him the prestigious position of personal bodyguard to the three-star general overseeing all troops in Somalia operations.

For his extraordinary service, Jim was hand-promoted to the rank of Sergeant by the Sergeant Major of the United States Marine Corps. But Jim wasn't done pushing himself. He decided to transfer to the United States Navy and pursue the rigorous Basic Underwater Demolition/SEAL (BUD/S) training, setting his sights on becoming a Navy SEAL.

Tragic Loss

Jim's relentless drive ultimately led to tragedy. While preparing for BUD/S, Jim would run 12 miles daily on base and practice 25-meter underwater crossovers. One fateful day, he pushed himself beyond his limits. During a training session, Jim suffered an underwater blackout and sank to the bottom of the pool. Despite efforts to save him, it was too late.

I was there when we got the call. The wind outside seemed to stop. The world stood still. The autopsy revealed that Jim had mentally pushed himself past his air capacity, a testament to his unyielding determination.

His loss left a void that could never be filled. But his memory lives on in the Marine Force Recon and Special Forces communities, where his story continues to inspire new generations.

A Brotherhood Beyond Words

Jim wasn't just a fellow Marine, he was a friend and mentor who profoundly impacted my life. One of my most cherished memories was attending BUD/S Class 180 graduation with Jim and Lance Dowd. It was there that our brotherhood transcended the physical, becoming something spiritual.

"Feels like we're being reborn," Jim whispered that day, as we watched these men complete one of the toughest training pipelines in the world.

When I transferred to 1st Force Reconnaissance Company, Jim and I crossed paths again. I had just returned from 3rd Reconnaissance Battalion after suffering a collapsed lung, a condition known medically as pneumothorax. My platoon sergeant sent me to the SCUBA Amphibious Dive Locker to work with a staff NCO whose reputation preceded him. There, I became the boat NCO, spending my days working on Del Mar Beach in the 21 Area of Camp Pendleton.

The ocean breeze was constant, salt mixing with diesel and sweat. Our uniform at the dive locker was as unconventional as our missions: Recon Surf and Sand which consisted of UDT shorts, Vietnam jungle boots, wool dive socks, Marine blouses, and covers. It was a reminder of the unique brotherhood we shared, a mix of grit, tradition, and pride.

"Where the mission ends, the brotherhood begins."

Carrying the Torch

Jim Burns was the original "Punisher" before the symbol became popularized. His strength, resilience, and dedication set a standard that I strive to uphold every day. Jim's legacy is etched into the very fabric of the Marine Corps and the Special Forces community. Though his life was tragically cut short, his spirit lives on through those of us who were privileged to know him.

Jim "The Body" Burns will never be forgotten.

"Legends don't die—they forge warriors in their wake."

On The Left, Lieutenant General Robert B. Johnston with (Then) Corporal Jim "The Punisher" Burns, on The Right.

Chapter 9

The Ceremony That Changed Everything

As a Marine, there are moments that define not just your career, but who you are at your core. For me, one such moment came on December 17, 1989, during the infamous Gold Wing Ceremony. It wasn't just a rite of passage—it was a brutal trial by fire, a test of loyalty, endurance, and spirit. What happened that day would leave scars both seen and unseen, changing the course of my life in ways I never could've imagined.

By then, I had served alongside some of the most elite warriors in the Recon community—brothers forged in hardship, bonded through pain, sweat, and shared purpose. One of them was company gunnery sergeant, a man who knew me not just as a fellow Marine, but as a person—my strength, my resilience, and what I stood for. He was there that day and later put into words what I could never fully express. The following is his firsthand account.

"The sun beat down hard over Subic Bay, the kind of heat that clings to your skin and burns straight through your uniform. It was December 17, 1989. The political chaos in the Philippines had finally settled down, and with tensions eased, the 3rd Recon Battalion gathered outside the gates of Subic Bay Naval Station for a tradition that few outside our world would understand—the Gold Wing Ceremony.

I remember standing by the door of the tavern,

watching Marines file in, laughing, joking—but their eyes said something else. We all knew what was about to happen. Nobody said it out loud, but everyone knew who was getting pinned hardest that day.

This wasn't for show. It was a blood ritual, a rite of passage earned through grueling jumps and punishing Recon training. The ceremony took place at a run-down tavern, the kind of place that reeked of spilled beer, sweat, and history. Marines filled the room—some there to be pinned, others to witness. Among the new recipients was Sergeant David James.

David stood out—clean white T-shirt, eyes locked forward, calm but ready. He'd earned those wings through grit and grind, and today, he'd wear them not just on his uniform, but in his flesh.

The ceremony began with the standard brutality. Each Marine took their gold jump wings, pressed the pins against their chest, and slammed them in using their Kevlar helmets. Blood followed. Tradition demanded it. It was painful, yes—but it was quick. That is, until David stepped up.

The Platoon Sergeant—a towering brute of a man with a reputation for cruelty—locked eyes with David. You could feel the tension in the room shift. He didn't just see a Marine about to be pinned—he saw a target. He wanted dominance.

I remember leaning to the Marine beside me and whispering, 'This is going too far.' But we all stood there, frozen, watching the kind of moment that makes or breaks a man.

The first punch came hard. Straight to David's chest, driving the wings deeper. Another. And another. Each blow more savage than the last. David staggered but didn't fall. That seemed to enrage the Platoon Sergeant even more. He screamed for a weapon rock—a jagged, 20-pound stone. One of the junior Marines hesitated, but returned with the rock.

What happened next felt like it moved in slow motion. The Platoon Sergeant raised the rock above his head and brought it crashing down on David's chest. The sound—flesh, metal, bone—was sickening. Marines jumped in, grabbing the Sergeant before he could strike again. David, somehow still conscious, was helped to a barstool, struggling to breathe. His shirt was soaked with blood. The room had gone from loud to eerily silent. The line between tradition and assault had just been shattered.

I will never forget the look on his face. Not pain. Not fear. Just determination. As if even through broken ribs, he refused to give the man the satisfaction of seeing him fall.

In the aftermath, David's pain only worsened. It wasn't until days later that medical exams revealed the extent of the damage—cracked ribs, a punctured lung, and a pneumothorax. The man we'd known as indestructible had been broken, not by war, but by one of our own.

The Platoon Sergeant was disciplined, demoted, removed from his post. But for David, the loss was far greater. The injuries stole from him the physical edge he had built his career on. Runs, rucks, water entries—all became reminders of what had been taken from him in that moment of cruelty.

Still, David never complained. Never cursed the system. He carried on, wounded but unyielding. That's what separates men like him."

That day could've ended me. Physically, it almost did. But spiritually—it marked the beginning of a deeper understanding. At the time, I couldn't see the purpose in that kind of suffering. But now, looking back, I can. God was there in the pain, in the chaos. He didn't stop the blow, but He gave me the strength to survive it—and the resilience to rise after it.

There's a difference between being knocked down and being taken out. That day knocked me down. But I got up. Because Marines don't quit—we adapt, we overcome, and we keep moving forward.

The scars I carry from that day aren't just from pins or punches or rocks. They're symbols of a greater journey. They remind me of who I became in that moment, of what it means to be broken but not defeated.

Company gunnery sergeant's testimony wasn't just paperwork for a claim. It was a lifeline. It validated the truth. It made sure the story of that day didn't get buried under the weight of silence. For that, I'll always be grateful.

I've prepared for combat, jumped from planes, and swum in the black waters of the Pacific—but nothing tested my identity like that ceremony. And nothing gave me more clarity about who I really was.

The Gold Wing Ceremony didn't just mark the end of my jump training—it marked the beginning of a new path. One paved with pain, yes—but also with purpose. One I was born to walk.

You don't get to choose how your defining moment shows up. But you do get to choose how you rise after it. And that's where your legacy begins.

Chapter 10

Presidential Navy and Marine Corps Medal For Heroism

It was a Saturday evening, and I had decided to stay on base rather than head out to the usual 1st Force Reconnaissance Company hangouts, the Sandbar in Carlsbad or the Beachcomber in Mission Beach, San Diego. These were our weekend spots, where the SDSU (San Diego State University) girls and us FORCE RECON and SEAL Team guys would hang out. But that night, something told me to stay back.

Sometimes, you do not know why you make a decision — until it saves someone else's life. That night, staying back wasn't a choice. It was providence.

Around 5:30 p.m., the duty Non-Commissioned Officer (NCO) knocked on my barracks door with urgent news: the dam on base had collapsed after three days of relentless torrential rain across Southern California and a Light Armored Vehicle (LAV) with its crew was stranded in the raging waters.

At the time, I was working in the 1st Force Reconnaissance Company [FMF] DIVE/SCUBA Locker as the Boat NCO under SSGT Vince. Most of the Recon Marines were out in town, but a few of us were still on base. Without hesitation, I took charge, assembled a team, and coordinated with a High Mobility Multipurpose Wheeled Vehicle (HUMVEE) driver and two other Marines. We rushed to Del Mar (21 Area) Camp Pendleton to the DIVE Locker, where we prepped the F-470 Zodiac boats, engines, fuel, and dive gear, including wetsuits, in anticipation of a rescue mission.

Meanwhile, the duty NCO was making calls to command and senior Staff NCOs, informing them of the situation.

The Rescue Mission

As we moved toward the stranded Marines, we linked up with other personnel heading to the flooded area. The damage was immediately evident. The raging waters had torn through the helicopter landing zone, submerging millions of dollars' worth of Marine Corps helicopters. Roads were underwater, with 12-foot-high palm trees barely visible above the surface.

You train for hardship. You prepare for the worst. But nothing prepares you for the moment when the enemy is water — cold, fast, and without mercy.

My team quickly offloaded the boats and launched into the rushing current. The scene was chaotic. As we approached, I spotted two Marines stranded on top of their nearly submerged vehicle. Maneuvering carefully through the fierce current, I steered our boat towards them and pulled them to safety.

"Hang on!" I shouted over the roar of the water as one of the Marines reached for my hand. "I've got you," I said, locking eyes with him. "You're not going under today."

We then turned toward a Landing Assault Vehicle (LAV), where three more Marines were trapped, standing helplessly on top of the vehicle, waiting for rescue. The current was relentless, and the operation was dangerous, one wrong move, and we could capsize. I grabbed one Marine, pulling him into the boat, while the other two quickly followed.

With all five Marines onboard, I carefully navigated back to safe ground. The current fought us the whole way, but we made it. The mission was a success.

The silence when we made landfall wasn't relief — it was awe. We didn't cheer. We checked gear, checked faces, and nodded. That's how warriors say "we made it."

After securing the rescued Marines and ensuring their safety, my team returned to the DIVE/SCUBA Locker to stand by for further orders. We remained on alert, geared up and ready for three more days.

The Aftermath

The following day, we deployed our two-man [SAS] Kayaks to patrol the river, searching for missing personnel and lost gear. We examined submerged vehicles, ensuring no one was trapped inside. For three days, we combed the area, retrieving bodies, equipment, and remnants of the flood's destruction.

Each kayak patrol brought new sights: wrecked metal, torn camo netting, broken helmets — reminders that this was more than water. It was devastation. We didn't stop. Not for rain. Not for exhaustion. That's what Recon does.

You go until it's done.

After four intense days of rescue operations, my team and I finally stood down. We were exhausted but proud of what we had accomplished.

Recognition for Valor

I [ETS] (End of Term of Service) from the Marine Corps on July 26, 1993, returning to my hometown of Apple Valley, Minnesota. After an unfortunate bar fight incident with an individual, I decided to leave Minnesota and relocate to Neenah, Wisconsin, to start fresh and be closer to my family.

Two years later, while still adjusting to civilian life, I attended the November 10th United States Marine Corps Birthday Ball at Menasha Germania Hall. After the Commandant's message and the traditional cake-cutting ceremony with the NCO sword, Marines from Platoon Sergeantous units stood to introduce themselves.

When it was my turn, I proudly stated my service: Force Reconnaissance Marine, Airborne Ranger, 1st Force Recon Company.

I stood tall when I spoke. Not for attention — but because I carried the weight of every Marine I had pulled from that flood.

After the ceremony, a 1st Sergeant from the Green Bay Naval and Marine Corps Reserve Unit approached me. He informed me that the Marine Corps had been looking for me to present an award for heroism. He instructed me to contact him, as the unit commander in Green Bay wanted to formally present me with the Presidential Navy and Marine Corps Medal.

A few days later, my father and I drove to Green Bay, Wisconsin. In a formal ceremony attended by 116 Navy and Marine Corps personnel in dress blues, the battalion colonel presented me with the Presidential Navy and Marine Corps Medal for Heroism.

The Citation Reads:

Sergeant James received the Presidential Navy and Marine Corps Medal for Heroism

While serving as Amphibious Boat Non-Commissioned Officer, 1st Force Reconnaissance Company; 1st Surveillance, Reconnaissance, and Intelligence Group; I Marine Expeditionary Force; Marine Forces Pacific; Camp Pendleton, California, from January 17 to 20, 1993.

With no notice for swift water rescue teams, Sergeant James assembled teams in response to an emergency call to rescue a Light Armored Vehicle (LAV) crew stranded in the swollen and raging Santa Margarita River.

While enroute to rescuing the stranded crew, off-duty Marines in a privately owned vehicle, disregarding high-water barricades, sped through the Vandegrift/Stuart Mesa intersection and submerged their vehicle in the flooding currents.

Sergeant James quickly adapted and rescued the trapped Marines from the roof of their disabled vehicle. Maneuvering through the violent, unknown waters, dangerous undertows, and submerged obstacles and debris, he recovered both the LAV crew and its communication equipment.

By his courageous and prompt actions in the face of great personal risk, Sergeant James reflected great credit upon himself and upheld the highest traditions of the Marine Corps and the United States Naval Service.

Signed by:

Secretary of the United States Navy

Commandant of the United States Marine Corps

A Reflection on Fate and Faith

Praise the Lord for putting me in the right place, at the right time, with the right people.

I rarely talk about this incident, but when I reflect on it, I realize how powerful and humbling it was to save those Marines from perishing in that flood. It was a soul-touching experience, one that will always stay with me.

What I saw that night wasn't just water — it was chaos, it was crisis, it was life and death. And what we brought back weren't just bodies — they were brothers.

I am deeply proud of my actions that day. But above all, I thank God for giving me the warrior spirit and protective soul that guided me through it.

In war, we wear armor. In peace, we carry memory. This medal hangs on my wall — but the moment it came from lives in my blood.

COMMANDANT OF THE MARINE CORPS

The President of the United States takes pleasure in presenting the
NAVY AND MARINE CORPS MEDAL to

SERGEANT DAVID D. JAMES
UNITED STATES MARINE CORPS

for service as set forth in the following

CITATION:

For heroism while serving as Amphibious Boat Noncommissioned Officer, 1st Force Reconnaissance Company; 1st Surveillance, Reconnaissance, and Intelligence Group; I Marine Expeditionary Force; Marine Forces Pacific; Camp Pendleton, California, from 17 to 20 January 1993. With no-notice for swift water rescue teams, Sergeant James assembled teams in response to an emergency call to rescue a Light Armored Vehicle crew stranded in the swollen and raging Santa Margarita River. While enroute to rescuing the stranded crew, off-duty Marines in a privately owned vehicle, disregarding high water barricades, sped through the Vandegrift/Stuart Mesa intersection and submerged their vehicle in the flooding currents. Sergeant James quickly adapted and rescued the trapped Marines from the roof of their disabled vehicle. Maneuvering through the violent, unknown waters, dangerous undertows, and submerged obstacles and debris, he recovered both the Light Armored Vehicle crew and its communication equipment. By his courageous and prompt actions in the face of great personal risk, Sergeant James reflected great credit upon himself and upheld the highest traditions of the Marine Corps and the United States Naval Service.

For the President,

Commandant of the Marine Corps

*The Presidential Navy and Marine Corps Medal Signed
By Commandant of The Marine Corps Charles C. Krulak.*

Chapter 11

My Saving Grace and Mentor: Senior Chief Mike Pardue, Seal Team One

WestPac 1988 was an experience that would shape me forever. It was an era defined by old-school Frogmen, where toughness was the standard, and weakness had no place. Amidst it all, one man became my saving grace, Senior Chief Mike Pardue of SEAL Team One. While we were on floating aboard the USS Ogden (LPD 5), Senior Chief Pardue handed me a book that would change my life: the Alcoholics Anonymous book, often referred to as "Mr. Bill's AA Book," along with the twelve steps to recovery.

Our platoon's mission during that deployment was basic reconnaissance, while Bravo Company (B Co) focused on CQB (Close Quarters Battle), HRT (Hostage Rescue Team), and Direct-Action (DA) missions. SEAL Team One, true to its legacy, handled it all. We departed from Long Beach Naval Base, California, heading west toward Okinawa, Japan. Life aboard the Ogden wasn't exactly thrilling. Most of our days were filled with PT (physical training), training classes, and, most importantly, staying out of the way of the Navy crew who kept the ship running.

We kept to ourselves, slept in tight quarters, and ate quickly. Nobody wanted to be the Marine getting called out by a boatswain for being in the way. Discipline wasn't optional — it was survival.

After 21 long days at sea, we finally reached Okinawa. There, we executed a boat insertion and ran a small recon operation, just the beginning of our WestPac tour. Over the next several months, we moved through 13 countries, training and operating in each. One mission stood out above the rest, our joint training with the Australian SAS (Special Air Service Regiment) in Perth. These commandos, modeled after the British SAS and living by the motto "Who Dares Wins," pushed us to our limits. After three grueling weeks of training, we were rewarded with five days of liberty in Fremantle and Perth.

That liberty turned into an alcohol-fueled blur, the kind where five days feel like one long, chaotic night. On the final day, I barely made it back to the ship before the midnight deadline, or so I thought. As I reached the top of the gangway, SSgt Oldham stood waiting. According to him, I was five minutes late. I argued; he pushed back. Tempers flared, and before I knew it, I had thrown the Staff Sergeant onto the flight deck. The next thing I remember, Navy Shore Patrol had me in handcuffs, dragging me down to the ship's berthing area. They cuffed me to a handrail, leaving me there for the night, stewing in a toxic mix of anger, embarrassment, and a pounding hangover.

That night felt longer than any mission I had been on. No sound, just the hum of the ship and the weight of my decisions pressing down on me.

The next morning, the Office in Charge (OIC) addressed the entire ship's crew and special operators, announcing that a Marine had been handcuffed in the berthing area after an altercation with a Staff NCO. It was humiliating, definitely not the kind of attention I had hoped to earn.

That's when Senior Chief Mike Pardue stepped in. He came down to berth, unlocked the cuffs, and without a word, led me to the ship's well deck. We ended up in the SEAL Team One dive locker, surrounded by scuba gear, the scent of saltwater and grease thick in the air.

He looked at me with calm eyes, the kind that had seen hard roads and harsh outcomes. "I've been where you are," he said quietly. "And if you don't change course, you won't like where it ends."

He handed me a copy of the AA Big Book and started talking. He told me about his own battles, how he had been just like me: a fighter, a hard drinker, and a hardcore operator. His drinking had spiraled so far out of control that the Special Warfare Command had kicked him out of the SEAL Teams. But he didn't let that define him. He fought his way back, filed a motion for reinstatement, and after a year of clawing his way up, he earned his place back in the Teams.

Mike's message was clear: if I didn't change, I wouldn't just lose my position as a reconnaissance Marine, I'd lose everything. He told me he had spoken with the ship's captain and my platoon sergeant, arranging for weekly AA meetings with him in the barber shop. That night, he planted a seed. And over time, it took root. I started to see that quitting drinking wasn't just about survival in the Corps; it was about reclaiming control over my life.

I still remember our first meeting in that barber shop. Just me, him, a coffee pot, and silence. "You don't need to talk yet," he said. "Just listen. Listening's a good place to start."

After our six-month deployment, Mike and I stayed in touch. At Naval Special Warfare (NSW) Base Coronado, he took charge of the BUD/S rehabilitation platoon, mentoring other operators who were struggling to find their way back. Even as life pulled us in different directions, his lessons stayed with me.

Years later, I reconnected with Mike through social media. He never mentioned he was battling cancer. That was just the kind of warrior he was, facing every challenge with quiet strength and unwavering determination. Shortly (Or a few years/months) after we reconnected, four years ago, he passed away. But his legacy remains alive in me. I am sober today because a true warrior cared enough to intervene.

Mike didn't save my rank. He saved my future. He didn't show me how to avoid pain. He showed me how to carry it without being crushed by it.

Senior Chief Mike Pardue may be gone, but he will never be forgotten.

His leadership wasn't in the medals or the title. It was in the moment he showed up when I was at my lowest — and chose not to walk away.

Us Navy Seal Joseph Schmidt.

Chapter 12
Motorcycle Crash and God's Divine Intervention

4.23.2009—13 Years and 1 Day Later After Jim's Passing

I was riding a Heritage Classic Harley Davidson after a Special Operations Bravo One Reunion. I was on the highway in Andrews, NC, going 70 miles an hour. As I approached a left-hand turn, I hit a pothole and went into a high-speed wobble. That's when it happened, I crashed into a steel guard rail.

I didn't even have time to pray. No time to think. One second I was on the bike, the next I was airborne—completely at the mercy of gravity, steel, and fate.

The impact was brutal. I was thrown 38 feet over the guard rail, landing hard and broken. My tibia was sticking out of my left leg in an open compound fracture. I was in and out of consciousness, overwhelmed by shock and pain. When I came to, I could see the chaos around me, four and a half units of my blood were pooling on the ground, staining the pavement and my brothers' hands. They worked frantically, using my belt as a makeshift tourniquet to stop the bleeding from the gash in my right leg.

I saw one of my brothers' faces—it was pale, locked in total focus. "We're losing him," someone said. I wanted to respond. I couldn't. I was already slipping.

My brothers called 911, demanding a life-flight helicopter. They knew I wouldn't make it otherwise. When the helicopter arrived, landing on the highway, the EMTs quickly loaded me onto a gurney. They kept talking to me, reassuring me as I drifted in and out of awareness. The reality of my injuries and the severity of the situation loomed heavy.

When we landed on the hospital's rooftop, the nurses and doctors rushed me inside. A priest walked up to my bedside, reading me my last rites. I remember the gravity of that moment, the weight of what wasn't being said. Survival mode kicked in, my Marine instincts refused to let go. But the medical team decided to put me in a medically induced coma to stabilize my condition.

Even as the drugs pulled me under, I had one final thought before the darkness took me: "God, if you're not done with me, then get me through this."

My Marine Reconnaissance brother, MADRECON, stayed in my hospital room for seven days, never leaving my side. Word of my accident spread quickly through our community. With the internet and Facebook, my Special Operations Warrior brothers from around the world called Mark's phone for days, offering their support, prayers, and positive energy to keep me fighting.

Warriors fight with rifles. But these men fought for me with faith. They circled me with strength I didn't have in my body—but felt in my soul.

After 36 days in the hospital and intensive

rehabilitation, I had to learn how to walk again. Tasks as simple as getting on and off the toilet or taking a shower were impossible at first. My rehabilitation specialist, April, played a crucial role in my recovery. She pushed me when I thought I couldn't go further, motivating me with her no-nonsense attitude and relentless encouragement. Thanks to her, I started moving again, slowly reclaiming my independence.

"I've seen Marines give up," she told me one day. "Don't be one of them." That hit me harder than any PT drill. I wasn't just healing—I was being re-forged.

The crash changed my life forever. It was a horrific accident that required months of recovery, six months in a wheelchair, another six on crutches. But it also led to an unexpected opportunity. My friend Lance Dowd, a retired Marine Force Recon Major, called me one day. He told me to pack my gear and head to San Antonio, Texas. There, Soldiers' Angels and their S.A.V.E. program gave me a job working with Wounded Warriors from Fort Sam Houston BAMC Medical Hospital. I found purpose again, sending care packages to men and women in combat zones and helping others heal.

What began with shattered bones ended in renewed calling. Pain had stripped me down—but service rebuilt me.

Looking back on that day, it's impossible not to see God's hand in every detail. From the belt used as a makeshift tourniquet to the arrival of the helicopter, every step of my rescue and recovery was filled with evidence of His divine intervention. I shouldn't have survived, but by His grace, I did. Even in my most broken state, God surrounded me with people who refused to give up on me.

It wasn't luck. It was alignment. Timing. Mercy. God didn't stop the fall—but He placed the right hands around me when I landed.

The crash taught me that life is fragile and fleeting, but it also reminded me of the strength and resilience that comes from faith. As I lay in that hospital bed, broken and battered, I felt an undeniable pull toward something greater, a reassurance that God wasn't finished with me yet. The opportunity to work with Wounded Warriors became more than a job; it became my ministry, a chance to share my story and help others find hope and healing.

Though I still carry the physical scars, I see them as reminders of God's faithfulness. That day could have been the end of my story, but instead, it became a new beginning, a testament to His power to bring purpose out of pain. Through every challenge, His grace has been sufficient, and His plans have proven far greater than my own.

I should've died on that highway. Instead, I woke up with a mission. Not to just survive—but to serve. That's how you honor a second chance.

Picture of The Author Two Hours Before Crashing on His Heritage Harley Into A Steel Guard Rail and Having His Last Rites Read to him by The Priest.

Chapter 13

The Incredible Journey of Pushing The Envelope of High Adrenaline and Serious Fitness and The "Gold's Gym" Experience!

In 1996, after getting out of jail and completing all the court-ordered rehabilitation programs, I started to focus on my total mental and physical rehabilitation. I was on a quest to regain confidence and apply my well-earned special operations positive attitude and never-quit mentality to my future and the opportunities ahead.

There was no manual for rebuilding your life after the chaos of the past and a jail cell. But I knew one thing for certain—motion is medicine. Discipline is freedom.

I gravitated toward physical fitness, which I had excelled at in the United States Marine Corps. I began working out with specific goals to achieve mental and physical conditioning and build pure confidence. My regimen included running, swimming, biomechanical weight training, and biking instead of driving. On top of working full-time in the physically demanding concrete business, I progressively started working out seven days a week for five hours a day to avoid returning to negative environments, such as bars, and risking getting into trouble again.

Most guys worked out for aesthetics. I trained like my life depended on it—because in many ways, it did. The gym wasn't a hobby. It was a battlefield where I chose to win each day.

The first goal I set for myself was to swim across Lake Winnebago, a 7.5-mile distance from South Park in Neenah, Wisconsin, to High Cliff State Park. My story of serving in special forces as a Force Reconnaissance Marine began to spread within the community, leading to coverage by the local papers, The Post Crescent and Northwestern, as well as local news. They highlighted my time in special forces and my Navy Marine Corps medal for rescuing five Marines during a major flood at Camp Pendleton.

After months of intense physical training, I was ready for the swim. I chose early May 1989 for the challenge. Friends, family, and local news came to support me. The cold water, a byproduct of the lake's paper mill pollution, felt healthier, as it could kill bacteria and other contaminants. To prepare for the freezing water, I coated my arms and legs with Vaseline. The thick layer was meant to provide insulation and reduce chafing from the constant friction of the water. Despite the protective barrier, I could still feel the sharp, icy bite each time the waves splashed against my skin. The wind that morning whipped across the lake, creating waves that made the water appear more like a restless ocean than a tranquil lake. As I waded in, the 3mm shorty wetsuit clung tightly to my body, offering some protection but not enough to shield me completely from the icy grip of the water. Each step into the lake felt like a descent into another world, a world that demanded everything from me both physically and mentally.

I didn't see it as just a swim. I saw it as a confrontation—with weakness, with fear, with everything inside me that still felt unfinished.

As I began, the rhythm of my side stroke settled in. The first mile felt smooth despite the choppy waters. By mile two, I could feel the cold starting to penetrate deeper, stiffening my limbs and slowing my strokes. Each breath brought in sharp air, and every wave that hit my face felt like a slap, forcing me to recalibrate my focus.

At approximately the 3-mile mark, I was beginning to show signs of hypothermia. My fingers felt numb, and my movements became sluggish, as if I were swimming through molasses. My friends in the safety boat could see I was struggling. They waved me over, but I shook my head, determined to press on. However, my energy reserves were depleting rapidly, and I knew I needed to refuel. Reluctantly, I allowed the boat to pull alongside me.

They handed me a ham sandwich and a bottle of water. My hands trembled as I took a bite, the simple act of chewing feeling like a monumental task. The warmth and energy from the food began to revive me. My friends' encouragement renewed my resolve, and I pushed off the boat, determined to finish.

One stroke at a time. That was my only goal. Not speed. Not form. Just movement. Forward.

The remaining miles were grueling. Each stroke felt

heavier than the last. The water's cold seeped into my core, making every movement a test of willpower. At times, I felt as though I were moving backward, the choppy waves pushing against me. I began reciting a mantra in my head, a rhythm that matched my strokes: "One more, just one more."

When I finally saw the shoreline of High Cliff State Park, a wave of emotion overtook me. The cheers of my friends and family carried across the water, mingling with the sound of the wind. I dug deep for one final push, my muscles screaming in protest. As I emerged from the water, my body was entirely blue, and my veins stood out like a roadmap. Even my lips were tinged with the color of hypothermia. My mother rushed to embrace me, her warmth and pride providing the comfort I needed after the grueling ordeal.

The swim had taken 6 hours and 10 minutes, but it felt like a lifetime. Exhausted yet exhilarated, I stood on the shore, knowing I had overcome one of the toughest physical challenges of my life. The media captured the moment, and my story was shared, inspiring others to push their limits. With that goal achieved, I immediately set my sights on a new adventure: preparing for my first bodybuilding show.

I didn't want sympathy. I wanted a standard to rise to. I didn't just want to recover—I wanted to compete.

I began training at the Neenah YMCA, learning about nutrition, biomechanics, and choreographed posing routines. Preparing for the bodybuilding stage gave me the discipline and focus needed to stay on track and transition from my military mindset. This commitment became a crucial part of my recovery journey from alcohol, keeping my mind and body occupied with positive goals rather than destructive habits. Months of training culminated in the Fox Valley Bodybuilding Show. Nervous but excited, I performed my 90-second routine in front of 500 people, weighing in at 154 pounds in the lightweight class.

I placed fifth in my weight class, and unbeknownst to me, the owners of the new Gold's Gym in Appleton, Wisconsin, were in the audience. Impressed by my positive attitude, they offered me a position as a personal trainer. I was certified in nutrition and biomechanics by Billy Smith from American Gladiators, officially becoming a Gold's Gym personal trainer when it opened on April 15, 1999.

In every athlete I trained, I saw a version of myself— someone fighting a quiet war inside and trying to win it one rep at a time.

While working at Gold's Gym, I poured my energy into helping others achieve their fitness goals. My schedule was relentless, often working 80 hours a week, balancing personal training sessions, teaching classes, and preparing for bodybuilding shows. Even with this intense workload, I remained committed to my own physical pursuits. Alongside bodybuilding competitions, I trained rigorously for endurance events, running five Fox Valley marathons and completing two triathlons. These grueling challenges demanded strict time management, discipline, and unwavering focus, reinforcing the mental toughness I had honed in the military. Every achievement, whether on stage or on the racecourse, pushed me further along my path of personal recovery and growth.

In 2000 I was blessed to meet a member of the gym, Jaime. Focused and serious about training, Jaime became the best training partner I could've ever asked for and still a great friend to this day! Her dedication and positive energy inspired me, and she excelled with my guidance in nutrition and biomechanics. Jaime's success became a testimonial to my training methods, and she continues to live a healthy, fitness-focused lifestyle to this day.

After a couple of years at Gold's Gym, I moved back to Southern California in 2003, reuniting with my special ops brothers at First Force Reconnaissance Company. Camp Pendleton was nearly deserted, as the First Marine Division was deployed to Iraq. With only $300 and no place to stay, I turned to the labor hall in Oceanside, California, and secured a construction job.

That first night sleeping in my car didn't feel like failure. It felt like a waiting room—just me, God, and the next chapter I had to earn.

For eight months, I lived in my car, parking at rest areas along I-5 near Camp Pendleton. The nights were long and often cold, with the hum of passing cars and the occasional sound of footsteps keeping me company. I would wake up early each morning, around 4:30 AM, and drive to the nearest LA Fitness to shower and clean up before heading to the construction site. The rest areas, with their sparse amenities and constant activity, were a stark contrast to the luxurious Southern California beaches I enjoyed on weekends. Despite these challenging conditions, I found moments of inspiration in my surroundings. One of my favorite places was Gold's Gym Venice, often called "The Mecca of Bodybuilding." This iconic gym, famously known as Arnold Schwarzenegger's home gym and featured in the documentary Pumping Iron, embodied the ultimate in fitness motivation. On other weekends, I would visit McP's Irish Pub in Coronado, enjoying the camaraderie and reflecting on the journey I was undertaking. In every sweat-soaked rep at Venice or moment of silence at McP's, I reminded myself— pressure creates diamonds, but first, it crushes rock. My employer, John, recognized my strong work ethic and kept me consistently busy, which allowed me to save money and stay focused on building a better future.

After a year, I returned to Wisconsin and worked at Madison's Gold's Gym, which was not only voted the best in the world at the time but also renowned for its cutting-edge facilities and vibrant atmosphere. The gym featured a state-of-the-art fitness juice bar, a $175,000 DJ booth blasting motivational music, and some of the best equipment available. This electric environment inspired me to go above and beyond in engaging members. I organized a skydiving event to bring the community closer and push everyone beyond their comfort zones. Over two weekends, 61 participants experienced the unforgettable thrill of skydiving, many for the first time. The excitement of freefall, combined with the camaraderie of sharing the experience, created lifelong memories. Afterward, we gathered for barbecues, exchanging stories of triumph and exhilaration. These moments solidified the gym as not just a fitness center but a place of growth, connection, and transformation.

Eventually, the gym was sold, and I moved back to Minnesota, working in concrete construction. After two years, I returned to Appleton, Wisconsin, where I rejoined Gold's Gym in corporate sales. Here, I discovered my true calling: mentoring youth and preparing them for military special operations. I had walked the fire. Now it was my turn to help others navigate it—with less pain and more purpose.

God's purpose for me was unfolding, leading to one of the greatest blessings of my life.

The Author Visiting Basic Reconnaissance Course (Brc) Naval Special Warfare Base Coronado, California as Students are Preparing to Conduct Helo-Casting Into The Ocean.

Chapter 14
Recovery, Transformation, and The Special Operations Mentoring Project Challenge

Life has a way of breaking you down before offering a path toward redemption. My journey of recovery and transformation began with hitting rock bottom and climbing my way back, one grueling step at a time.

A Rocky Road to Recovery

Losing my driver's license was the wake-up call I didn't know I needed. For a year and a half, I relied on my trusty California beach cruiser to get around. It wasn't easy, but it forced me to slow down and reflect. During this time, I developed an obsession with fitness. Exercise became my escape, my therapy, and my way of taking control of my life. Swimming across Lake Winnebago, lifting three-hundred-pound weights, running marathons, and competing in triathlons were more than physical challenges, they were milestones in rebuilding myself.

Every mile I ran, every iron plate I lifted, wasn't about looking strong. It was about proving to myself that I still was. That I could endure. That I could overcome.

This newfound discipline landed me a job at Appleton, Wisconsin's "Gold's Gym" as a personal trainer and nutritionist. Working at the gym wasn't just about fitness, it became my springboard for inspiring others. It was here that the seeds of what would later become the *Special*

Operations Mentoring Project Challenge were planted.

Unconventional Jobs and Rediscovering Confidence

During my years of self-reinvention, I took on some unusual roles. For four years, I worked as a nude model for the art department at Appleton Community College. It was strange at first, but it helped me regain confidence in myself and my body. This eventually led to being featured in *Playgirl* magazine, which further fueled my self-assurance.

Funny thing was, standing under harsh studio lights or on glossy magazine pages felt less vulnerable than admitting my failures. Sometimes exposing your body is easier than exposing your scars.

With this newfound confidence, I embarked on a two-year stint as a male stripper. I performed at events, earning decent money that often ended up funding wild nights out at the Top Hat Martini Bar. My training partner, Jaime, and I would cruise around in rented Cadillac Devilles, living the high life after my gigs. It was a whirlwind, but it taught me a lot about showmanship and pushing personal boundaries.

Skydiving Adventures

Skydiving was another outlet for my boundless energy and thrill-seeking nature. From Minnesota to Fort Atkinson, Wisconsin, I hopped out of planes with Bo and Alex, the owners of Aphorisms Sky Dive. One of my most daring moments was skydiving naked at the Black Creek Sky Dive Club, a wild experience reserved for club members only. These adventures kept me grounded in an odd way, helping me see life from a different perspective, literally.

Falling thousands of feet through the air strips life down to what matters most—heartbeat, breath, faith. Up there, it's just you and gravity. And God decides the rest.

The Move to California

In 2003, I decided it was time for a fresh start. I packed up my car, "Beverly Hillbillies" style, with just $300 in my pocket and no job waiting for me. Living on baloney sandwiches and sleeping in my car for four days, I made my way to sunny California. Driving down the 405 freeway toward the Pacific Coast Highway, I felt an overwhelming sense of peace seeing the ocean once again.

It wasn't the coastline that settled me—it was the whisper that said, "You're exactly where you need to be."

My first stop was Camp Pendleton, home to 1st Force Reconnaissance Company. I wanted to reconnect with my recon brothers. The base was bustling, preparing for deployment to Iraq. I caught up with "Chilly Willy" and some old friends, but I knew my next priority was finding work and a place to sleep.

I reached out to Major Lance Dowd, who welcomed me into his home. He and his wife, Holly, paid for a hotel room for me in San Clemente for a few nights while I figured things out. The next morning, I drove to a labor office in Oceanside and put my name on the list for day labor jobs. After working a few days for a heavy equipment operator named John, I secured a full-time job with his construction company in Valley Center, California.

Living in Survival Mode

For the next year, I lived out of my car, alternating between rest areas along the I-5 North and Southbound highways. I slept in different spots each night to avoid being noticed by state troopers. Living this way wasn't glamorous, but it fueled my determination to build a better future. It reminded me of the grit and resilience I'd developed during my years in the military.

I was back in a form of deployment—only this time my foxhole was the driver's seat, my MRE was a gas station sandwich, and my orders were simple: survive, rebuild, repeat.

This chapter in my life reflects a period of growth, perseverance, and rediscovery. Every challenge and unconventional job brought me closer to becoming the man I needed to be, a man ready to inspire others through the Special Operations Mentoring Project Challenge. It's proof that even in our lowest moments, the fire within can guide us toward greatness.

It wasn't always pretty. It wasn't always noble. But it was necessary. And it forged me into someone who could look a young man in the eye, tell him what it takes to be a warrior, and mean every word.

Chapter 15

From Special Operations To GORUCK and Mentoring Troubled Youth

Mentoring the Next Generation of Special Operations Candidates

W hile working with Basic Reconnaissance Course (BRC) and mentoring MARSOC candidates preparing for Marine Corps Special Operations Community A&S Program and U.S. Naval Special Warfare BUD/S, I dedicated time to training Marines in tactical swimming and conditioning. I attended S.O.I. BRC and MART twice a week to help these Marines pass the rigorous selection process and become 0321 Recon Marine Operators.

Nothing matched the look in their eyes when they realized they'd conquered something they once thought was impossible. It wasn't just pride — it was ownership of their future.

Joining GORUCK: The Special Forces Civilian Challenge

It was during this time that I heard about GORUCK, a civilian special operations-inspired organization that developed military-grade rucksacks, designed and field-tested at Fort Bragg, the home of U.S. Army Special Warfare. Beyond gear, GORUCK had created grueling military-inspired fitness events led by active-duty and retired special forces operators with at least eight years of service in elite units, primarily Green Berets.

I was hired by the GORUCK Ops Chief, a retired Master Gunnery Sergeant who was widely respected throughout the Marine Recon Community, known as "Big Daddy". Before leading events as Cadre, I had to complete a brutal Indoctrination (INDOC) by participating in a full event. Once I officially joined, my life revolved around traveling across all 52 states and internationally, leading some of the toughest civilian challenges in the world.

I remember standing there before my first GORUCK INDOC, the American flag snapping in the wind, thinking — this is where leaders are forged beyond the base. Same principles, different kind of challenge.

The GORUCK Experience: Pushing the Limits

Every weekend, I flew to different states or countries, from California to London, leading GORUCK Heavy, Tough, and Light (HTL) events. These challenges pushed participants, primarily CrossFit athletes, firefighters, police officers, SWAT units, and military veterans, to their absolute limits.

The events lasted up to 72 hours, with minimal sleep and food. Participants endured extreme physical conditioning, carried logs, performed special operations calisthenics, and endured cold-water training. Each participant wore the GORUCK GR-1 rucksack, weighing 35 lbs or more, depending on class size.

I worked alongside elite special operations veterans, Army Green Berets, Navy SEALs, Force Recon Marines, and Airborne Rangers, teaching leadership, resilience, and teamwork.

We didn't just break their bodies — we rebuilt their minds. We showed them where the wall was, then taught them how to climb over it.

9/11 GORUCK Showcase – A Life-Changing Experience

One of the most humbling moments of my career came when I was selected to lead the GORUCK 9/11 Showcase Event in New York City. With 518 participants, we started at the top of Manhattan, retracing the timeline of September 11, 2001.

We stopped at firehouses and police precincts, paying tribute to the fallen first responders. As Cadre, we led participants through New York City, teaching leadership and teamwork, ensuring they met strict timelines. The event culminated at the shoreline in front of the Statue of Liberty, near Ground Zero.

When we paused for the moment the towers fell, the crowd went silent. Even hardened police officers and combat vets had tears. I whispered a prayer: "Lord, let them feel why we carry these burdens."

As we honored the exact moment the Twin Towers fell, remembering the brave firefighters, police officers, and civilians who perished, I felt an overwhelming sense of humility and gratitude. It was one of the most powerful and emotional experiences of my life.

The Demand of a Life on the Road

For two years, I lived out of hotels, rental cars, and airports, leading GORUCK events across the country and abroad. Every weekend, I conducted brutal events, coordinated logistics, training routes, and safety measures. I loved seeing ordinary people transform into resilient leaders, taking on challenges that shaped them into entrepreneurs, CEOs, and stronger individuals.

Watching them stumble under a log, then stand straighter with each mile — that's why we did it. Because that kind of grit follows you long after the ruck is gone.

A New Path: Mentoring Troubled Youth

When COVID-19 shut down the country, GORUCK operations came to a sudden halt. I found myself back in Appleton, working temporarily at a NAPA auto parts store. During this time, I was contacted by a retired U.S. Army Sergeant Major who had seen my bio and résumé through the Veterans Unemployment Office.

He asked if I was interested in becoming a Team Leader for a youth program. I had never heard of the program but was intrigued. The hiring process was rigorous, involving three interviews over several months. With the Lord's guidance, I was finally hired as a Team Leader.

The program is a 5 ½-month quasi-military course, giving troubled teens a second chance to earn their high school diploma, learn discipline, leadership, and teamwork, and prepare for a better future.

The cadets live in WWII-era Army barracks. They train in physical fitness, rappelling off a 55-ft tower, swimming, weight training, and confidence-building exercises. When they make poor choices, they carry sandbags and logs to reinforce the reality of accountability and consequences.

Sometimes they'd glare at me, thinking I was the enemy. I'd tell them, "I'm not here to punish you. I'm here to show you how to carry your own weight — so the world can't break you later."

Drawing from my own experiences in the military and special operations, I help them develop resilience, overcome struggles, and push past mental barriers. But instead of yelling or intimidating, I lead with understanding and guidance, helping them learn from my hardships and mistakes.

Their scars were different from mine — not from injuries you could see, but from homes that failed them. I wanted to show them what it looked like to fight for yourself.

A Calling Beyond the Military

Through this program, I have seen young men and women transform their lives, moving from despair to hope, from failure to success. My military past, special operations training, and years as a mentor have all led me here, to this mission of serving others.

I am truly blessed to have this opportunity, and as long as the Lord continues to guide me, I will never stop motivating, leading, and pushing others toward their highest potential.

I once carried a rifle. Now I carry stories. I once fought to survive. Now I fight to help others live. And in that, I have found my highest ground.

Never Quit – Look to God for True Strength

The Author with Marine Recon Brother Rudy Reyes at Naval Special Warfare Swim Tank Coronado, California.

The Author During His Time As Goruck Cadre in Chicago, Illinois Getting The Participants Wet Cold and Sandy, Known as "Sugar Cookies".

The Author With Us Navy Seal Joseph Schmidt at Mission Beach During Goruck in San Diego, California

Sowmpc Special Operations Warrior Mentoring Project Challenge Candidates Training in and on The Beaches of The Pacific Ocean on Camp Pendleton, California.

Chapter 16

My Closest Special Operations Brother: Corpsman John "Jack" Walston, Navy Seal

My connection with my brother, John "Jack" Walston, ran deep. Our paths first crossed in 1986 when he checked into our unit, and from the start, there was something magnetic about him. John had the classic California surfer vibe—blond hair, a lean and powerful physique, and a bright, infectious energy. He radiated positivity and passion for life, and though he was technically assigned to Bravo Company and I was in Charlie, we quickly became close friends.

We bonded through our shared fire for fitness, challenge, and pushing limits. In our early days, we'd often cruise into Los Angeles, tearing up Sunset Boulevard near Beverly Hills, absorbing the high-energy atmosphere and dreaming bigger. John—"Doc Walston" to us—served as a Navy Corpsman with the Marines and quickly earned the respect of every man in the unit. We worked together during WESTPAC 88 aboard the USS Ogden LPD-5. After that, our bond only grew stronger. John, and I pushed each other through brutal workouts, grinding side-by-side to become faster, sharper, and mentally stronger.

In 1989 John wrapped his time with 1st Reconnaissance Battalion. John, originally born in Madrid, Spain but raised in La Porte, Texas, threw himself into the world of elite endurance—competing in professional cycling races with the same intensity he brought to everything.

John's next chapter was forged in fire. He re-enlisted in the Navy with one target in mind: becoming a Navy SEAL. While he endured the crucible of BUD/S training, I was stationed at 1st Force Recon, working the dive locker. I visited him a few times in Coronado, and he never failed to deliver a story—often wild, always laced with his quick wit that cut through the misery like sunlight.

When BUD/S Class 180 graduated, John's tight-knit group of Marine buddies drove down to witness and share John's immense achievement. The sun blazed down on Naval Special Warfare Center, and the energy in the air was electric. A seasoned SEAL delivered a thunderous speech on the Warrior Ethos. When John received his gold Trident, he also earned the "Fire in the Gut" award—recognized as the most motivated candidate in the class. He was the guy who cracked jokes at the worst moments, when everyone was wet, cold, and near breaking—reminding them that laughter, too, is a weapon.

Before arriving at SEAL Team Four on the East Coast, John completed the elite 18 Delta combat medic training at Ft. Sam Houston. From there, he worked multiple times at Central and South America. His reputation only grew. John spent nine years in the Navy—half of it with Marine Corps 1st Recon and the other half with SEAL Team Four in Little Creek, Virginia.

John had married his soulmate, Teri, in 1992, and

they honeymooned in Israel, grounding their relationship in shared faith. They built a strong, purpose-driven life in La Porte, Texas, raising five children together. In 1997, John and Teri launched one of the first civilian mentorship and bootcamp-style fitness programs inspired by Naval Special Warfare. "The Original SEAL PT Course" changed the game.

Their programs were brutal, transformative, and deeply spiritual. From the youth "Tadpole" course to high-octane adult challenges, the movement caught fire—drawing in astronauts, Olympic athletes, and elite professionals. John's leadership and magnetic spirit even earned him the honor of carrying the Olympic torch through Houston, Texas.

They later expanded into international adventures—Belize, Costa Rica, Panama—merging jungle expeditions with life-altering leadership training. These weren't just trips—they were missions. Cave diving, horseback riding, leadership drills, and at the end of the day, they'd gather under the stars at a jungle-themed bar to debrief with food, laughter, and stories that lit the fire in every soul present.

Teri and John also launched corporate and team-building programs, helping organizations, sports teams, and companies tap into deeper resilience, grit, and cohesion. Meanwhile, I was launching my own youth mentoring program. Our bond never faded. We spoke often—sometimes for hours—about faith, growth, and our shared mission to raise warriors for the next generation.

John was old-school toughness meets deep heart. As a SARC Corpsman, Navy SEAL, and lifelong sailor, he taught with purpose. Whether leading evolutions in wet, cold, and sandy environments, or teaching how to navigate the open ocean, John demanded the best—and got it.

But after years of giving everything, the weight of his service began to press heavy. On February 6, 2020, when I was alerted to John's sudden passing due to complications related to undiagnosed mesothelioma, I was devastated. The news hit like a gut punch. I dropped everything and drove straight to a Catholic church, lit a candle, and prayed for Teri and the kids.

We honored him with a warrior's farewell in Galveston—SEALs, Marines, family, and friends gathered to pay tribute. His ashes were spread into the Gulf of Mexico, the same waters that once brought him peace. Later, his name was read among the fallen at the Navy SEAL Museum. A public celebration of life at the Houston Yacht Club followed, complete with military honors, a cannon shot, and the raising of both the American and Spanish flags.

I think about John often. I still talk to Teri and keep up with his kids. His legacy lives on in my work with the Youth Challenge Academy, where I share his story with every cadet who walks through our doors.

He is never forgotten. Always in my heart. His legacy lives in every cadet I train, every challenge I lead, and every story I share. Jack Walston will always be part of the mission.

The Author, Lance, and Jim at John's UDT/SEAL BUD/S Graduation, Class 180, Naval Special Warfare Base, Coronado, California.

Chapter 17
What It Takes To Mentor Our Youth Into Special Forces Operators, and Great Americans

I have been fortunate to spend over 25 years mentoring youth, preparing, educating, and motivating the next generation of Special Warfare operators. Many of these young men and women come from challenging backgrounds, some lacked the guidance and support they deserved during their formative teenage years. It has been my mission to help fill that gap.

I always believed God didn't bring me through hardship, jail, near death, and recovery just to stand still. He brought me through it to stand beside them.

What it Really Takes to Mentor Youth

True mentorship requires more than just instruction. It starts with earning their trust, showing them that what you say is grounded in truth and experience, and more importantly, that you live by the very lessons you teach. Understanding everyone's needs and unique situation takes time, patience, and a keen ability to read the subtle signs that others may miss.

Over my two-plus decades as a mentor, I've learned how to recognize those signals and address each situation with the right balance of firmness and compassion. It's about making genuine connections, so they know you care. Often, this means helping them reframe how they process their emotions and teaching them discipline, guiding them to respect themselves, their peers, and their team. When they begin to operate as one unit, accomplishing tasks and solving problems together, they start to grow.

I've watched a kid who couldn't hold eye contact on day one become the one pulling his buddy to safety on day thirty. That's transformation you can't fake.

As a leader and mentor, you must always set an example, without exception. Youth are incredibly perceptive; they are constantly observing to see if you practice what you preach. Your integrity and consistency become the blueprint for them to follow.

When I worked with the United States Marine Corps and Navy Delayed Entry Programs, building a respectful and trusting relationship with each candidate was essential. Listening to them was just as critical as leading them.

In the world of Special Warfare mentorship, safety is paramount, especially in aquatic environments where risks escalate quickly. My program was 80% water-based, conducted in both pools and open oceans. I pushed my candidates hard, but always with an uncompromising eye on safety. They treaded water for over two hours with weights around their waists and in their hands. They dove 15 feet on a single breath to retrieve gear, completed underwater crossovers up to 50 meters, and learned to stay calm under extreme conditions.

You'd hear them gasping after a drill, their chests heaving, eyes wide — and I'd lean down and say, "This is where most people quit. So decide right now: are you most people?"

These scenarios were not without danger, shallow water blackouts are a constant threat. I lost my Force Recon brother, Jim "The Punisher" Burns, to such a tragedy. His loss added intensity to my purpose. I became even more vigilant, ensuring my candidates were well-trained, mentally tough, and never placed in unnecessary danger. Mentoring them in these high-stress environments required more than just technical knowledge; it demanded sharp instincts, attention to detail, and relentless focus.

I would stand poolside, scanning every ripple, every hesitation. Because I wasn't just training future operators. I was safeguarding someone's son. Someone's brother. Someone's only hope.

As mentors, we must be masters of what we teach. Safety and success go together. For Special Warfare candidates, the challenge is as mental as it is physical. They must develop an unbreakable "never-quit" mindset, one that will carry them through the grueling pipelines of Special Operations training and into the ranks of an elite brotherhood.

It's not just about who can swim the farthest or run the fastest. It's about who refuses to fold when pain sets in, when doubt starts whispering. That's what we forge.

Mentorship also requires command presence. From

the very first interaction, they must feel your confidence, see your level of fitness, notice your attention to grooming, and hear your respect when you speak. First impressions matter. So do the lasting impressions you leave when your time with them comes to an end.

Integrity and reputation are everything. They are the currency that earns you the privilege of shaping young lives and securing opportunities to serve as a mentor and leader to our future warriors.

I am grateful for the path my life has taken. I have been honored to run my own mentoring programs for Marine Corps Special Operations and Naval Special Warfare candidates across the globe. From my time as Cadre at GORUCK, standing shoulder-to-shoulder with former Special Operations members from every military branch, to conducting programs in Wisconsin, Minnesota, Texas, California, and beyond, the journey has been humbling and rewarding.

Sometimes I think back to sleeping in my car, or standing in a jail cell, or bleeding on a highway — and I'm reminded that redemption isn't a gentle road. It's a road earned through scars.

That's why I pour everything into these young men and women. Because I know what's on the other side if they don't learn to fight for something better.

Sowmpc Candidates Running at Camp Pendleton Usmc Beach.

Chapter 18
What I Learned About Mentoring Our Youth

What I've learned over the years is that no matter their backgrounds, dreams, or circumstances, every young person is blessed with unique attributes, skills, and passions. Deep down, they all want the same thing: to live a productive, meaningful life.

Some just don't know how to get there yet. That's where we come in.

As a coach, mentor, or instructor, your role is to help them unlock that potential. It takes patience. It takes being a great listener and having a toolbox of experiences to pull from so you can handle any challenge that comes your way. Mentoring is incredibly rewarding, you get to witness growth firsthand as they mature, develop discipline, build courage, and learn the power of teamwork. These are the pillars of success.

Watching that first spark — when a kid realizes he's stronger than his excuses — that's why you keep showing up.

An important lesson I've learned is to "know your swim lane." As a mentor, coach, or leader, you must ensure that the information and guidance you provide is clear, accurate, and tailored to your team, whether it's an individual, a small unit, or an entire platoon. It's your job to be their compass, helping them make smart decisions, instilling the value of proper nutrition, rest, and recovery, and teaching them how to regroup before the next evolution of training.

Sometimes it's about telling them, "Get your head on straight, fuel up, tomorrow we hit it harder." Because growth isn't just pain. It's process.

Mentoring is not just about pushing hard every single day. It's about balance. You need to motivate, uplift, and reward them. You need to look them in the eye and tell them how proud you are.

For example, when my Special Operations candidates completed my program, whether I mentored them for two years or six months, depending on their ship dates to Boot Camp, I always gave them a unique reward. To celebrate their grit and determination, I would take them tandem skydiving. We'd jump from 2.5 miles up, freefalling at 122 miles per hour. It was my way of honoring their commitment to never quitting and always pursuing their dreams.

At 13,000 feet, there's no room for doubt. Just faith, gravity, and trust that you did the work. It's why I loved that final test. It was raw truth.

A good mentor also sacrifices. I've invested my own time and money to give my mentees the best chance of success, whether that meant a YMCA membership, fuel costs, or equipment.

Knowledge is power. The more you teach, the more prepared they'll be, not just physically, but mentally and emotionally. And no one can mentor alone. I made sure to create partnerships with others who could support the mission. For instance, I trained my Special Operations candidates heavily in aquatics, in pools, open water, and oceans. At the YMCA in Appleton, Wisconsin, I built strong relationships with the lifeguards. I kept them fully informed about the intensity of our water-based training so they could step in if needed. I also made them part of the journey, explaining our goals and helping them feel invested in what we were accomplishing.

It wasn't just my mission. It became our mission. And when they graduated, it felt like everyone had earned it.

A mentor must sweat the details, hydration, proper gear, safety, and even morale. In the Midwest winters, no matter how brutal the cold, we trained outdoors for hours. Freezing temperatures just sharpened their mental toughness and resilience. Whether it was calisthenics, rucking, or long-distance running, the goal was always to teach them to endure, no matter the conditions.

I'd tell them, shivering, breath hanging in the air, "If you can learn to be comfortable here, you'll crush it anywhere life sends you."

Safety was paramount. First aid kits, proper lighting for night evolutions, flotation devices, reflective gear, every scenario required preparation. And as a mentor, you must always be thinking ahead, always protecting them, while also pushing them past perceived limits.

I was fortunate to spend five years mentoring on

Camp Pendleton's Del Mar Beach, working with the U.S. Marine Corps' MWR/MCCS program. The towering Pacific surf, the endless sand, it was the perfect setting to challenge my candidates and teach them grit, resilience, and a "never quit" mentality.

There's something about the roar of the ocean under moonlight, surf crashing as kids bury logs into wet sand, that burns itself into your soul. It's where warriors are born.

For me, faith has always been a silent partner in my mentorship. I never force it, but I show my mentees that there's a Higher Power guiding them, especially in those moments when the water tests their limits. I teach them to be comfortable in uncomfortable situations, to stay calm, cool, and collected when the pressure rises.

When they came up gasping after a long underwater drill, I'd say quietly, "There's grace in every breath you get. Remember that."

A good mentor is also aware of the world around them. I paid close attention to where our military forces were deploying, the environments they were facing, and the types of battles they might encounter. Knowing these details meant I could better prepare my Special Warfare candidates to survive and succeed, and God willing, to come home safely.

Mentoring isn't just about preparing them for service, it's about preparing them for life after the military. I always encouraged my mentees to think long-term, to seek education, and to build a future beyond their uniforms. For the younger youth I mentor, I guide them toward career paths and life paths that will empower them to be strong parents, leaders, and contributors to society.

I also lived by the motto "One Team, One Fight." I collaborated with other programs, Navy SEAL mentors, Green Berets, Marine Special Operations instructors, to share resources and create a unified mission: to help our youth rise to their fullest potential.

The uniform may change, the state flag may change, the patch may change — but the mission never does. It's to lift each other higher.

Through all my travels, all the mentors I've worked alongside, and all the young men and women I've coached, one truth stands out: mentoring the next generation is one of the most important things we can do. If we each give a piece of our time to invest in them, our nation will thrive. The youth are the torchbearers who will keep the beacon of light burning in this great country, the United States of America.

At the end of the day, mentoring our youth is about leaving a legacy of resilience, service, and hope. It's about being the person who shows up, who believes in them, who pushes them to be more than they thought possible. These young people are the future leaders, protectors, and builders of our country. If we can guide them to stand tall, to persevere, and to lead with integrity, then we've done our part to ensure that the light of this great nation keeps shining. And that is what I carry with me every single day.

I may not have chosen every chapter of my life — but I choose this: to pass the torch, so their future burns brighter than my past ever did.

Chapter 19
The Torch We Carry

As I reflect on my journey, from the early days of standing on the yellow footprints to becoming a mentor for the next generation, I've come to realize that the calling to serve never truly ends. The uniform may eventually come off, but the mission continues. It shifts, it evolves, but its purpose remains the same: to make an impact, to leave the world better than you found it.

Throughout my years coaching, mentoring, and leading, I've witnessed the incredible transformation that takes place when young people are given the tools and belief to push past their limits. Whether it was a young recruit learning how to trust themselves in frigid waters or a candidate finding their grit under the weight of a ruck in freezing conditions, I've seen them all grow into warriors, leaders, and contributors to something greater than themselves.

The lessons I've passed down, resilience, discipline, faith, teamwork, courage, are more than military values. They are life values. They are the foundation of a life well-lived, a life of service, a life of purpose.

But what I've learned most is this: mentoring is not a title or a job, it's a responsibility. It's a lifelong mission to guide, protect, and inspire the next generation, regardless of where you are or what role you hold.

I've carried a rifle. I've carried a Bible. Now I carry stories — and the weight of making sure they're told right.

That's also service.

It's also a calling rooted in faith. For me, it was the Lord who carried me through the darkest nights, the toughest challenges, and the loneliest roads. Every trial I faced, whether in service or while guiding others, only deepened my relationship with God. It was through Him that I found the courage to keep showing up, to lead with purpose, and to be a light for others.

The world outside can be chaotic. The youth coming up today are facing pressures and distractions that can easily derail them. They need mentors, role models, and people willing to invest the time and energy to guide them. Whether you wear a uniform, coach a team, or simply lend your ear to someone who's struggling, you are holding a torch.

It's the torch of leadership, service, and belief.

Sometimes that torch feels heavy. But every time you lift it up for someone else to see, you push back the darkness just a little more.

We don't always know where our influence will end or how far it will ripple. Sometimes it's the smallest acts, the quiet words of encouragement, the shared moments of struggle, the steadfast presence when times get tough, that leave the greatest mark.

I've seen young men and women who were once uncertain and unfocused go on to become leaders in their own right, SEALs, Force Recon Marines, MARSOC Raiders, or simply better citizens in their communities and families. That is the power of mentorship.

As you close this book and step back into your own life, I ask you to consider this: Who can you mentor? Who can you lead? Where can you make a difference?

Our youth are watching, learning, and waiting for someone to show them the way. Be that person.

Because at the end of the day, it's not just about the miles we've run, the battles we've fought, or the accolades we've earned. It's about the legacy we leave, the faith that has sustained us, and the future we help build.

It's about teaching them to be the kind of person who will pick up someone else's pack when they're too tired to carry it themselves. That's the real mark of a warrior.

Keep pushing forward. Keep giving back. And always trust that God is walking beside you, as He always has with me.

One Team. One Fight. Under God. Always.

Dave "Rage" James

Sowmpc Special Operations Warrior Mentoring Project Challenge Candidate.

Chapter 20
Forged From The Fire

Throughout my journey, I've had the blessing of standing shoulder-to-shoulder with some of the most extraordinary warriors this world has known. Men who not only sharpened my edge in the heat of battle, but shaped my soul in the silence after the storm.

One of those men was Jim "The Punisher" Burns—a living legend in both the Force Recon and Navy SEAL communities. Jim carried himself with a commanding quiet presence. His mere walk through a ship's passageway would cause crowds to part like the Red Sea. His physique, demeanor, and laser-focused intensity earned him a reputation that few could rival.

Jim didn't need to say much—his actions spoke volumes. When he did speak, his words carried weight. Every mission, every moment was calculated. And as his brother, I studied everything—how he moved, how he thought, how he led. He poured wisdom into me, not through lectures, but through the way he lived.

The last time I saw him, we crossed paths outside the chow hall at 1st Force Recon. He stopped me mid-step, looked me in the eye, and left me with this:

"Stay in shape. Eat clean. Be ready for what lies ahead. And never follow the crowd—lead with what you've learned. Carry the torch. That's your next mission."

That torch has never left my hand.

Another was my brother John "Jack" Walston, a warrior with deep spiritual fire. John taught me that being a warrior for God was not something to hide—but something to celebrate. We'd spend hours talking on the phone, diving into the kind of deep spiritual territory most men never dare approach. He showed me that even in the darkest missions, against the fiercest enemies, we are never alone.

John's words still echo in my soul:

"Lead. Follow. Or get the hell out of the way."

He was direct. Demanding. But he taught me to train with purpose. To push others to their edge—not for ego, but to help them unlock their potential. He reminded me to never withhold the tools that could change someone's life. His legacy lives on in every young man I've mentored.

Together, John, Jim, and Lance were my brothers-in-arms. Our warrior ethos wasn't built on words—it was forged through pain, grit, and mutual respect. We lived the motto: *"The only easy day was yesterday."*

And then there was Senior Chief Mike Purdue, a Frogman from an era when things were tougher, harder, and less forgiving. Mike carried a calm confidence that spoke of depth. His guidance came during a time when I needed it most—when I was unraveling, searching for grounding.

Mike didn't just reel me back in—he reminded me of

the discipline, the poise, and the mission-focused mindset that makes a true warrior. His mentorship helped reshape how I lead others. Not with pressure—but with purpose.

Each of these men—Jim, John, Mike—helped refine the warrior and mentor I am today.

As I trained my own candidates through the Special Operations Warrior Mentor Project, I wove their lessons into every exercise, every story, every challenge. My students leaned in—eager, hungry to understand. They didn't just hear stories; they felt them. They lived them. And in doing so, they taught me as much as I ever taught them.

I stood at their graduations—humbled. Proud. Watching these young men transform before my eyes. I saw my mentors' fingerprints on every success, every breakthrough, every tear.

This book... it's not just about me. It's about all of them—my brothers, my cadets, my spiritual family. It's about a life lived in the trenches, and the power that comes from surviving the fire.

It's about battles I've fought both out there—and in here. Battles with depression, addiction, fear, and failure. It's about how I learned to rise, not by pretending I was fine—but by doing the work. The hard work. The healing work. The warrior work.

I am a sword—
Forged by flame.

Tempered by hardship.
Sharpened by brotherhood.
And held by the hand of God.

If you've made it to this point in the story, I hope you feel it—that you are not alone in your struggle. That through chaos and pain, through heartbreak and healing, there is always a path forward.

Keep finning.
Keep swimming through the surf.
And never forget—you are loved, and you matter.

Let this book be a torch you carry now—so that you too can light the way for someone else.

—David James, USMC

Picture With My U.S. Army Green Beret Brother By My Side

Pre-Mentoring Prep Course And Nutrition Program

Designed to help prepare for elite military special operations training courses.

Outline

1. Enlistment Confirmation – Verification of enlistment in the U.S. military.
2. Enrollment in Special Operations Pre-Screening Training Course – Introduction to the program.
3. Completion of Pre-Screening Training Course – Assessment of readiness.
4. MOS Contract Signature – Induction into the Special Warfare Pipeline.

Elite Covert Fitness Training: From the Spartans to Special Forces

Extended Prep Course (Pre-Screening Course)

Physical & Academic Evaluations:

- Physical Conditioning: Swimming, calisthenics, running, sit-ups, pull-ups.
- Academic Aptitude: Minimum 110 GT score.
- Training Structure:
- Minimum participation: Three days per week (Monday/Wednesday/Friday, 1700 hrs, 3 hours per session).
- Progression: Training difficulty increases weekly.

Day 1 – Waterborne Operations

- 1000m fin swim
- One-hour treading water
- "Ditch and Dons" (underwater equipment removal)
- Life-saving techniques
- Underwater crossovers, 'Sharking'
- Special Warfare side stroke & backstroke

Equipment:

- Duck Fins/Rocket Fins
- Goggles/Mask
- BDUs with combat boots
- 16 lb. weight belt
- Underwater brick, chem-lights

Day 2 – Underwater Demolition Calisthenics

- Push-ups, sit-ups, jumping jacks
- 12-count bodybuilders, bends & thrusts
- Pull-ups, running, open water 2000m fin swim

Day 3 – Review & Swim Buddy Training

- Recap of Day 1 & 2
- Safety protocols
- Swim buddy techniques

US Marine Force Recon / MARSOC Mentoring "Tadpoles"

- 500m swim (under 10 min, side/breaststroke)
- 7 pull-ups, 60 push-ups, 80 sit-ups

- 3-mile run (under 18 min)
- 3-mile rocket fin swim with dive mask & BDUs
- Pool bobbing & underwater demolition exercises

Underwater Demolition Short Card "Frog's Club"

- Side straddle hops – 4x25
- Marine Corps-style push-ups – 4x25x5 (Airborne, Scuba, Recon, Ranger, Special Ops)
- Bends & thrusts – 4x25
- Special Warfare flutter kicks – 4x25
- Windmills – 4x25
- Hello Dollies – 4x25
- Boot beaters – 4x25
- Sun gods – 4x25
- Mountain climbers – 4x25
- 8-count bodybuilders – 4x25
- Bend forward & aft – 4x25
- Up back and overs – 4x25
- 1.5-mile run or 500m swim with fins & mask

Underwater Demolition Long Card "US Amphibious Dual Action Team"

- Jumping jacks – 4x50
- Half jacks – 4x50
- Push-ups – 4x50
- Trunk twisters – 4x50
- Mountain climbers – 4x50
- Flutter kicks – 4x50
- Hello Dollies – 4x50
- Bend forward & aft – 4x50

- Sun gods – 4x50
- Boot beaters – 4x50
- 12-count bodybuilders – 4x50
- High jack / High low – 4x50
- Leg raises – 4x50
- Windmills – 4x50
- Marine Corps push-ups – 4x50 (Airborne, Scuba, Recon, Ranger, Special Ops)
- Bends & thrusts – 4x50
- Press flings – 4x50
- Navy Special Warfare flutter kicks – 4x100
- 6-mile run or 2000m open-water fin swim (Rocket Fins, Dive Mask, BDUs, Combat Boots)
- Gear issued: Scout Swimmer Equipment, Coral Booties, Duck Fins/Rocket Fins, UDT Vests
- Training in all weather conditions: rain, snow, hurricanes, tornadoes, earthquakes

The Nutrition That Makes Warriors

MEAL PLAN – EAT EVERY TWO HOURS

Breakfast:

- Oatmeal (plain) – 1 cup
- Cinnamon Raisin Bagel – 1
- Flavored Low-Fat Yogurt – 1 cup

Meal 2:

- 3 Whole Eggs
- 2 Slices Whole Wheat Bread
- Orange Juice – 1 glass
- Banana – 1

Snack:

- Flavored Yogurt – 1 cup
- Apple – 1
- Dry-Roasted Peanuts – ½ cup
- Water – 8 oz

Lunch 1:

- 98% Fat-Free Turkey Breast with Whole Wheat Bread & Low-Fat Miracle Whip
- Almond Butter (natural)
- Cauliflower – 1 cup
- Applesauce
- Unsweetened Orange Juice

Lunch 2:

- 98% Fat-Free Chicken Breast with Whole Wheat Bread & Low-Fat Miracle Whip
- Carrots – 1 cup
- Low-Fat Cottage Cheese – 1 cup
- Water – 8 oz

Snack:

- Celery – ½ cup
- Raisins – 1 cup
- Apple Juice – 8 oz

Dinner 1:

- Boneless, Skinless Chicken Breast – 1 whole
- Carrots – 1 cup
- Fat-Free Mozzarella Cheese
- Flavored Non-Fat Yogurt – 1 store cup
- Grapefruit Juice – 8 oz

Dinner 2:

- Haddock – 1 ½ servings
- Green Beans – 1 cup
- Brown Rice – ½ cup
- Water – 8 oz

Dinner 3:

- Water-Packed Tuna with Whole Wheat Bread & Low-Fat Miracle Whip
- Brown Rice – ½ cup
- Broccoli – 1 cup

- Cantaloupe – 1 slice
- Grapefruit Juice – 8 oz

Snack:

- Mixed Fruits (Grapes, Raspberries, Pears, Kiwi, Apricots)
- Mixed Dry-Roasted Nuts – ½ cup
- Cashews – ½ cup
- Natural Peanut Butter – ½ cup with Honey Nut Rice Cakes
- Water – 8 oz

EVERY TWO HOURS – NO EXCEPTIONS!

DO YOU HAVE THE HEART TO BE FIT?

Nutrition Plan by David James ⌜SEP⌝ Certified Personal Trainer

Faith, Grit, And Mentorship, Lessons From A Marine Who Turned Warriors Into Leaders.

Life and Times of Rage

The Journey of Special Ops Mentorship, Marine Force Recon

One Team. One Fight. One Mission, Our Youth

Through the eyes of Marine Force Reconnaissance veteran Dave "Rage" James, *Life and Times of Rage* takes you deep inside the world of Special Operations mentorship. From the beaches, the weight room to freezing waters, this is a story of grit, discipline, and unwavering service.

Guided by faith and driven by purpose, Rage shares hard-earned lessons from decades of leadership, training elite Special Ops candidates and mentoring youth from all walks of life. His mission has remained constant: prepare them for life's toughest challenges and ensure they never quit.

More than a personal journey, this book is a call to action. Packed with raw experiences, powerful insights, and a deep love for his country, *Life and Times of Rage* inspires us all to invest in the next generation and carry the torch forward.

About The Author

David James is a USMC Force Recon veteran with over 25 years of experience mentoring youth and training Special Operations warriors. A lifelong servant-leader and man of faith, he has dedicated his life to shaping resilient, purpose-driven young men and women.

Praise For Life And Times Of Rage

"A powerful and inspiring book that shows how one man's faith and leadership shaped the lives of countless young warriors."

Rudy Reyes, U.S. Marine Recon Sniper, Actor (*Generation Kill* – HBO), Host of *Special Forces: World's Toughest Test* (Fox)

"The key to making it through Special Forces training is having a strong why, being a team player, and embracing the mindset that the only way out is in a body bag. Never quit! Rage, you're a great friend, servant leader, and warrior. I'm honored to know and serve with you."

Joseph Schmidt, U.S. Navy SEAL (Ret.), BUD/S Class __ *"The Only Easy Day Was Yesterday."*

"Rage pulls back the curtain on a life lived at the edge of human endurance. From combat swims and airborne jumps gone wrong, to the sacred brotherhood of Force Recon and the fight to find purpose after the uniform, this story is one of grit, pain, and redemption."

Major Fred Galvin, USMC (Ret.)

www.ingramcontent.com/pod-product-compliance
Lightning Source LLC
Chambersburg PA
CBHW020738130626
46554CB00006B/2039